Biomedical Data Science: A Step-by-step Guide to Analysis and Interpretation

Published 2026 by River Publishers
River Publishers
Broagervej 10, 9260 Gistrup, Denmark
www.riverpublishers.com

Distributed exclusively by Routledge
605 Third Avenue, New York, NY 10017, USA
4 Park Square, Milton Park, Abingdon, Oxon OX14 4RN

Biomedical Data Science: A Step-by-step Guide to Analysis and Interpretation / by Denis L. Cascino, Giovanni Gatti, Luca S. Matarazzo, Sandeep Unwith, Simone G. Riva, Giovanni Damiani, Andrea Tangherloni.

Routledge is an imprint of the Taylor & Francis Group, an informa business

ISBN 978-87-4381-246-3 (hardback)

ISBN 978-87-4381-476-4 (paperback)

ISBN 978-87-4381-249-4 (online)

ISBN 978-87-4381-248-7 (ebook master)

ISBN 978-87-4381-251-7 (ePub)

DOI: 10.1201/9788743812487

A Publication in the River Publishers Rapids Series in *Computer Engineering and Information Science and Technology*

Biomedical Data Science: A Step-by-step Guide to Analysis and Interpretation

Denis L. Cascino

Bain & Company, Milan, Italy

Giovanni Gatti

Bocconi University, Milan, Italy

Luca S. Matarazzo

Department of Computing Sciences at Bocconi University, Milan, Italy

Sandeep Unwith

University of Oxford, UK

Simone G. Riva

University of Oxford, UK

Giovanni Damiani

University of Milan, Italy and Case Western Reserve University, USA

Andrea Tangherloni

Department of Computing Sciences, Bocconi University, Milan, Italy

River Publishers

Routledge
Taylor & Francis Group
NEW YORK AND LONDON

Contents

Preface

Biomedical data science is an interdisciplinary field combining biology, statistics, and computer science. Over the past two decades, this field has undergone rapid evolution, driven by the increasing availability of high-throughput omics data, advancements in computational power, and a growing demand for reproducibility and interpretability in research.

This book is not intended to be a comprehensive technical manual; instead, it emphasises the fundamental principles of effective biomedical research. We guide the reader from the initial stages of experimental planning to advanced modelling techniques, using real-world examples and minimal jargon to make the contents accessible to readers coming from various disciplines. The final hands-on chapter provides a practical guide, illustrating how the methods discussed throughout the book can be incorporated into a cohesive and reproducible workflow.

We want to express our gratitude to our students and colleagues, whose questions, feedback, and challenges have significantly shaped the structure and content of this book. We also thank River Publishers for supporting the dissemination of practical and open scientific knowledge.

We hope this book will serve not only as a reference but also as a springboard for critical thinking and exploration in biomedical data science.

List of Abbreviations

AMS Acute mountain sickness

ANOVA Analysis of variance

ATAC-seq Assay for transposase-accessible chromatin using sequencing

AUC Area under the curve

BH Benjamini–Hochberg procedure

BMI Body mass index

CCS Case-control study

ChIP-seq Chromatin immunoprecipitation sequencing

CI Confidence interval

CRP C-reactive protein

CSS Cross-sectional study

CV Cross-validation

DAS28 Disease activity score in 28 joints

DBSCAN Density-based spatial clustering of applications with noise

df Degrees of freedom

DNase-seq DNase I hypersensitive sites sequencing

ENCODE Encyclopedia of DNA elements

FDR False discovery rate

FPKM Fragments per kilobase of transcript per million mapped reads

FWER Family-wise error rate

GMM Gaussian mixture model

HSD Tukey's honestly significant difference

ICU Intensive care unit

IL-6 Interleukin-6

k-NN k-nearest neighbours

LASSO Least absolute shrinkage and selection operator

LR Logistic regression

MAE Mean absolute error

ML Machine learning

MSE Mean squared error

NNs Neural networks

OR Odds ratio

PCA Principal component analysis

PPV Positive predictive value

RA Rheumatoid arthritis

RCT Randomised controlled trial

RF Random rorest

RL Reinforcement learning

RNA-seq RNA sequencing

ROC-AUC Receiver operating characteristic area under the curve

scATAC-seq Single-cell assay for transposase-accessible chromatin using sequencing

scRNA-seq Single-cell RNA sequencing

SD Standard deviation

SE Standard error

SOP Standard operating procedure

t-SNE t-distributed stochastic neighbour embedding

TFs Transcription factors

TNF-α Tumour necrosis factor-α

UMAP Uniform manifold approximation and projection

Introduction

In the mid-2000s, a promising cancer therapy reached the final stages of development. Based on cutting-edge genomic analysis, researchers believed they had found a way to personalise chemotherapy. By using gene expression data from patients' tumours, they were able to predict which drugs would work best for each individual. The data looked solid, the models were elegant, and the results were initially astonishing. Encouraged by these early findings, the work was fast-tracked toward clinical trials. Patients were enrolled, and treatments were assigned based on algorithmic predictions. It was a bold step forward, the kind of precision medicine that had long been the aspiration of modern oncology. However, then something went wrong . . .

As independent researchers attempted to replicate the original results, inconsistencies began to emerge. The models could not be reproduced, and predictions failed to generalise. Upon deeper investigation, it was discovered that critical steps in the data pipeline had been flawed from the beginning. Sample labels were misassigned, and the data had been preprocessed inconsistently and without documentation. Most damning of all, batch effects (i.e., systematic, non-biological variations introduced during laboratory processing) had been mistaken for biological signals. What appeared to be predictive patterns were, in reality, technical artefacts. The models were not discovering biology; they were capturing noise.

When the findings emerged, the clinical trials were halted. The reputational and financial damage was substantial. Years of work, millions in funding, and, most importantly, patients' time and trust had been compromised. What began as a hopeful vision of personalised medicine ended as a cautionary tale about data mismanagement.

This story was not a failure of technology. The tools were powerful, and the vision was sound. The problem was in how the data were handled (i.e., how experiments were designed, how preprocessing choices were made, and how assumptions went unchecked). In the rush to innovate, the principles of robust and reproducible science had often been bypassed.

This example is not an isolated incident. Across biomedicine, similar stories continue to emerge. There are high-impact studies that cannot be replicated, model predictions that fail in real-world settings, and data-driven claims that dissolve under scrutiny. These failures are not just statistical artefacts; they are preventable consequences of poor design, inadequate analysis, and a lack of appreciation for the nuances of biomedical data. The good news is that these pitfalls can be avoided.

This book is about getting it right.

Why Biomedical Data Science?

Biomedical data science sits at the confluence of biology, statistics, and computer science. It is an interdisciplinary applied discipline with a mission: to extract meaningful information from noisy, complex, high-dimensional data and use it to generate insights that improve human health. Extracting this information may involve understanding molecular mechanisms, identifying disease biomarkers, predicting patient outcomes, or evaluating treatment efficacy. It is clear that the potential is enormous, but the challenges are significant.

Unlike data in other fields (e.g., finance or retail), biomedical datasets often reflect biological variability, incomplete annotations, missing values, and complex dependencies among the variables. Moreover, the cost of mistakes is high: a misinterpreted signal might lead to a failed clinical trial, a missed therapeutic opportunity, or flawed public health guidance. To navigate this space, practitioners must understand the **biological** and **clinical questions** and **the data-driven methodologies** required to answer them.

From design to interpretation: a structured approach.

This book provides a structured, step-by-step guide to biomedical data science. We begin not with algorithms or code, but with the foundation of all good science: **experimental design**. The best Machine learning (ML) model in the world cannot recover from a poorly designed study.

Part I of the book emphasises how to plan robust, interpretable, and reproducible studies, whether using bulk RNA sequencing (RNA-seq), single-cell data, or epigenomic assays like Assay for transposase-accessible chromatin using sequencing (ATAC-seq) and Chromatin immunoprecipitation sequencing (ChIP-seq).

We then move to *Part II*, which introduces the statistical and ML techniques most relevant to biomedical applications. Rather than overwhelming the reader with technical derivations, we focus on conceptual understanding, assumptions, and use cases. Statistical tests are presented alongside Python code and real-world examples, enabling readers to apply each method immediately. Key ML paradigms (e.g., supervised and unsupervised learning, dimensionality reduction, and ensemble methods) are discussed, with a focus on biomedical-specific challenges, including imbalanced datasets, noisy labels, and the reproducibility crisis in predictive modelling.

Finally, **our book** ends up in a comprehensive, real-world case study that integrates the concepts from the previous chapters. The example is carefully chosen to reflect a typical analysis workflow in biomedical research: from study planning and preprocessing to statistical inference, modelling, validation, and interpretation. By the end, the reader will have followed a complete data science pipeline and developed an appreciation for how decisions at each stage influence the outcome.

Reproducibility, interpretability, and critical thinking.

Across all the sections of the book, we emphasise three main principles: **reproducibility**, **interpretability**, and **critical thinking**.

- **Reproducibility** is crucial to modern biomedical science. We discuss the causes of irreproducible results—such as p-hacking, publication bias, and hidden confounders—and offer practical strategies to mitigate them. These include maintaining transparent and executable workflows using code notebooks (which document every analytical step and parameter choice), setting random seeds, applying permutation tests, and adopting robust validation procedures such as nested Cross-validation (CV) or repeated random sampling.
- **Interpretability** is essential for biomedical applications. A black-box model with perfect accuracy is of limited use if it cannot be explained to clinicians or used to generate hypotheses. We highlight the importance of interpretable models and inductive biases, and discuss trade-offs between accuracy and transparency using examples from regression, decision trees, and regularised models.
- **Critical thinking** remains the most valuable skill in any scientist's repertoire. For instance, statistical significance is not equivalent to scientific significance; a good classification metric does not necessarily prove generalisability, and a correlation is not a mechanism. Thus, we encourage readers to ask themselves: *What assumptions am I making? What are the potential confounders? Could a simpler model work just as well? Is the result biologically plausible?*

Who is this book for?

This book is intended for **graduate students**, **postdocs**, **early-career researchers**, and **healthcare professionals** working at the intersection of biology, medicine, and data science. It is also suitable for **computer scientists** or **engineers** looking to transition into biomedical applications. Readers are expected to have a basic understanding of statistics and some experience with programming, but this textbook is designed to be approachable and self-contained.

Our goal is not to cover every possible method or tool but to provide readers with the core competencies needed to carry out rigorous and thoughtful biomedical data analyses. Wherever possible, we avoid mathematical abstraction in favour of clarity, examples, and actionable insight.

A note on tools and code.

The code examples in this book are written in **Python**, using widely adopted libraries such as NumPy, pandas, SciPy, scikit-learn, and matplotlib. These examples are not intended as production-ready scripts but as starting points for your exploration. In several cases, we highlight the role of visualisation in data science, not merely as a means of presentation, but as a vital component of understanding, debugging, and validating models. Wherever relevant, we also highlight existing datasets, public resources, and community standards that can serve as benchmarks for comparison and reference.

To promote transparency, reproducibility, and community engagement, all programming code presented in this book will be made publicly available through a dedicated GitHub repository managed by River Publishers [1]. Each code example in the text is linked to its corresponding location in the repository, enabling readers to access the complete, executable code.

This approach enables readers to reproduce analyses, extend the provided examples, and adapt the code to their own biomedical datasets. In addition, the GitHub platform provides a structured process for reporting issues, suggesting improvements, and offering feedback. This fosters an open and collaborative learning environment aligned with best practices in computational biomedical research. Readers are strongly encouraged to replicate the examples and modify them to explore alternative approaches.

[1] https://github.com/RiverPublishers/Computational-Approaches-in-Biology-and-Medicine

Looking ahead.

Biomedical data science is not a solved problem. It is a growing, dynamic field that continues to evolve as new technologies emerge and new questions arise. This book reflects the current state-of-the-art but also a philosophy: **rigorous thinking**, **careful design**, and **transparent analysis** will always be more valuable than the latest algorithm.

We hope that this guide serves as a **reference**, a **tutorial**, and a **source of inspiration**. Whether your goal is to publish robust findings, guide clinical decisions, or understand the methods behind the headlines, this book aims to support you at each step of the journey. Let us begin...

About the Authors

Denis L. Cascino is an associate consultant at Bain & Company, Milan, specialising in the Healthcare and Life Sciences Practice, jointly with the Private Equity Group. Before moving into strategy, he interned at Novartis Basel as an AI Engineer in biostatistics and advanced methodologies and has assisted Professors Tangherloni and Damiani with their research on psoriasis and male infertility.

Denis earned his B.Sc. in international economics and finance and M.Sc. in data science and business analytics from Bocconi University. He is passionate about the rapid development of AI in drug discovery and aims to explore the establishment of funds specialised in advanced life science methodologies.

Giovanni Gatti is a second-year MSc student in Artificial Intelligence at Bocconi University, Milan, in the Department of Computing Sciences. He is also a Visiting Research Student at the Computational Biology Lab within the same institution, as part of the BIDSA Visiting Students Initiative.

His research focuses primarily on the computational analysis of large-scale clinical data. Giovanni also has industry experience, having worked as a Software and AI Engineer in both large technology companies and startups.

Luca S. Matarazzo is a researcher in the Department of Computing Sciences at Bocconi University in Milan. His current research focuses on developing statistical and machine learning techniques to model multi-omic data for precision medicine applications. He earned his B.Sc. in economics and M.Sc. in data science from Bocconi University. Luca also has research experience in economics, particularly in empirical industrial organisation.

Sandeep Unwith completed his Ph.D. in molecular oncology at the University of Oxford, where his research focused on glucose and glycogen metabolism in triple-negative breast cancer. He was a visiting scientist and EuroAge Net Awardee, conducting computational research at Bocconi University and Oxford into RNA sequencing and chromosome conformation capture techniques. He holds a Joint Honours degree in biomedical science and business management from Imperial College London. His research and professional interests include cancer metabolism, biomedical data science, and innovation in the life sciences.

Simone G. Riva is a senior computational and machine learning scientist in genomics at the University of Oxford. As a computational biologist working at the intersection of computer science and genomics, he specialises in developing advanced machine learning models and bioinformatics pipelines aimed at exploring and decoding non-coding regions of the genome. His research focuses on designing high-throughput computational strategies to investigate complex genomic elements, including coding sequences, splicing mechanisms, regulatory networks, and structural features. By creating efficient and reproducible workflows and curating specialised datasets, he applies cutting-edge machine learning technologies to generate novel insights into genome biology, thereby bridging the gap between artificial intelligence and biological discovery.

Giovanni Damiani is an associate professor of dermatology at the University of Milan and a clinical professor at Case Western Reserve University (US). He holds a Ph.D. in pharmacology (2020–2024) from the University of Padua (IT), an M.Sc. in pharmacovigilance, pharmacoepidemiology, pharmacoeconomics, and real world evidence (2024–2025) from the University of Verona, Italy, and two postdoctoral positions in dermato-immunology (2018–2020) at Case Western Reserve University, and in the immunology of oral diseases (2020–2022) at the University of Milan.

As a dermatologist, he strongly believes in the "physician scientist" model, which combines clinical evidence and research to resolve challenging cases. He has developed his expertise in cutaneous immune-mediated diseases (i.e., psoriasis, hidradenitis suppurativa, and atopic dermatitis) and eco-pharmacovigilance.

His efforts materialised in 2019 with the establishment of the Italian Centre for Precision Medicine and Chronic Inflammation at the University of Milan, where various skilled professionals (i.e., biologists, bioinformaticians, doctors) collaborate to enhance daily practice through translational research.

Andrea Tangherloni is an assistant professor in the Department of Computing Sciences at Bocconi University, Milan. His research focuses on the intersection of artificial intelligence and the life sciences, aiming to develop novel computational methods to solve complex biological and medical problems. He integrates computational intelligence techniques (e.g., evolutionary computation, swarm intelligence, and fuzzy systems) with deep learning to develop efficient, interpretable tools for biomedical data analysis. His work covers multiple areas, including computational biology, systems biology, bioinformatics, biomedical image analysis, and single-cell omics.

Andrea earned his B.Sc., M.Sc., and Ph.D. in computer science from the University of Milano-Bicocca, where his doctoral research investigated the use of high-performance computing and AI to solve problems in systems and genome biology. He has held research positions at the University of Cambridge, the Wellcome Sanger Institute, and Bocconi University. His current work concentrates on integrating AI and biomedical data science to advance translational research and precision medicine.

Part I

Experimental Design in Biomedical Research: Principles, Methodologies, and Technical Optimisation

CHAPTER

1

Experimental Design

1.1 General Experimental Design Considerations

Careful experimental design is the foundation of reliable biomedical research. Given the complexity and heterogeneity of biological systems, no single experimental model can fully replicate the human body. As such, robust design is essential to ensure that the collected data are both meaningful and reproducible. Well-designed studies not only improve internal validity but also facilitate translation to advanced models or clinical trials.

This section highlights common pitfalls in experimental design and presents guiding principles to mitigate bias, improve reproducibility, and increase the real-world applicability of biomedical findings.

1.1.1 Randomisation

The process of randomisation (i.e., the random assignment of participants to different treatment or intervention groups) helps balance known and unknown confounding factors across groups, thereby minimising systematic bias in experimental results. However, in some cases, not all confounders are known or accounted for. A prominent example is a 2013 clinical trial, reported by Estruch *et al.* [1], conducted in Spain, which examined whether a Mediterranean diet could help prevent heart disease in individuals at risk. A later review uncovered significant randomisation errors affecting up to 1,588 participants. Some were

10.1201/9788743812487-2

assigned the same diet as their household members, a detail that was not initially reported. In rural areas, diet assignments were based on the nearest clinic rather than proper randomisation. These issues undermined the study's validity, demonstrating that flawed randomisation can introduce bias and potentially mislead conclusions, even in large-scale trials.

1.1.2 Control groups

Control groups are essential for assessing the effects of treatments or interventions, as they provide a baseline for comparison and serve as a standard against which to evaluate the impact of the treatment or intervention. Cell lines are laboratory-grown populations of cells that can be propagated for long periods under controlled conditions and are widely used as simplified, reproducible models of human tissues. However, in cell-line-based studies, which are only one of many experimental systems in biomedical research, creating contemporaneous controls can be challenging due to differences in genetic background, growth rates, and cell viability. In cancer research, truly normal primary cells cannot be maintained in culture for long periods because they have limited proliferative capacity. As a result, researchers often rely on immortalised but non-tumorigenic cell lines as surrogates for normal tissue, even though these models may not fully replicate the molecular characteristics of primary cells. For example, MCF-10A, a non-tumorigenic epithelial cell line, is frequently used as a model for normal human mammary epithelial cells, but it has genetic alterations that can affect signalling pathways. This raises concerns about whether MCF-10A truly represents normal cells, as evidenced by retracted papers highlighting discrepancies between MCF-10A and actual breast cancer tissues.

1.1.3 Appropriate statistical tests

The VITAL study was a large-scale clinical trial examining the effects of vitamin D and omega-3 supplementation on the prevention of cancer and cardiovascular disease [2]. One of its findings suggested a 28% reduction in heart attack risk with omega-3 supplementation, particularly among African American participants.

However, the study has been criticised for not adjusting for multiple comparisons, which increases the likelihood that some results occurred by chance. Experts suggest that statistical corrections, such as the Bonferroni adjustment, would strengthen the reliability of its findings.

Multivariate analysis is crucial in biomedical research because variables are often interrelated and complex in nature. For example, if a univariate analysis were used to assess risk factors for heart disease, including age, cholesterol levels, blood pressure, smoking status, Body mass index (BMI), physical activity, and family history, it would examine each factor in isolation, ignoring potential interactions among variables. In contrast, multivariate analysis reduces confounding effects, identifies interaction effects, and improves predictive accuracy.

1.1.4 Causality vs. correlation

Researchers must carefully consider the direction of relationships when concluding. Are the independent and dependent variables correctly assigned? In the early 2000s, a number of meta-analyses suggested a link between antidepressant use and increased suicide risk in adolescents, raising public concern, which was also included in the FDA's Public Health Advisory report, suggesting a black box warning label be added to all antidepressant medicines given to adolescents. However, it is argued that these studies failed to properly control for confounding factors such as the severity of depression and underlying psychiatric conditions, which could have contributed to suicidal thoughts regardless of antidepressant use. For instance, patients with more severe depression may be more likely to be prescribed antidepressants. Therefore, if we observe a higher risk of suicide among those taking antidepressants, it may reflect their underlying condition rather than the medication itself, creating a correlation between antidepressant use and suicide risk that does not imply causation. These concerns have been addressed by Lock *et al.* [3] and Goren *et al.* [4].

1.1.5 Blinding issues

Blinding reduces bias in data collection by ensuring that participants (single-blind) or both participants and experimenters (double-blind) are unaware of group assignments. Following a systematic review of a Randomised controlled trial (RCT), it was found that, by comparing blinded and non-blinded sub-studies by Hrobjartsson *et al.* [5], participant-reported outcomes were exaggerated by 0.56 standard deviations in non-blinded trials. The discrepancy was even greater in studies investigating invasive procedures. Various biases, including observer, performance, selection, attrition, reporting, and interview bias, can influence non-blinded studies, highlighting the importance of proper blinding.

1.1.6 Sample size determination

Determining the correct sample size is essential for detecting meaningful effects while minimising errors. However, challenges such as limited sample availability or high costs can lead to underpowered studies, reducing their reliability. If the sample size is too small, the study may lack sufficient statistical power to detect meaningful effects, increasing the risk of Type II errors (false negatives), where real effects go undetected. Additionally, small sample sizes can lead to high variability, resulting in higher uncertainty, which makes results less reliable and harder to generalise to a larger population. Limited sample availability or high costs often contribute to this issue, potentially leading to inconclusive or misleading findings.

1.1.7 Publication bias

Studies with positive or significant results are more likely to be published than those with negative or null findings [6]. This bias can lead to an overestimation of treatment effects in meta-analyses. RCTs with positive results are more frequently published, leading to exaggerated pooled effect sizes. While publication bias typically inflates findings, it can also obscure real effects, as seen in a meta-analysis of 25 RCTs by Schuch *et al.* [7], where publication bias led to an underestimated standardised mean difference between exercise and non-exercise groups on depression symptoms. All scientific research should be published regardless of whether the outcome is considered negative. The magnitude and direction of publication bias must also be carefully considered when evaluating scientific literature.

1.1.8 P-hacking

P-hacking, also known as data dredging, refers to the manipulation of data or analyses to achieve statistical significance, even if the results are not meaningful or reproducible [8]. This can involve selectively reporting findings, continuing data collection until significance is reached, or running multiple tests without proper adjustments. While many researchers engage in p-hacking without realising, it constitutes scientific misconduct, it can inflate false positive rates (Type I errors), exaggerate effect sizes, and undermine the reproducibility of biomedical studies.

1.1.9 The reproducibility crisis

Poor study design, including inadequate controls, lack of randomisation, bias, selective reporting, and p-hacking, has contributed to a reproducibility crisis in biomedical research. Begley *et al.* [9] highlighted that more than 90% of preclinical cancer drug studies failed to reproduce.

Addressing the issues highlighted above is crucial for enhancing the reliability of biomedical research and ensuring that findings can be effectively translated into real-world applications.

1.2 General Experimental Design Considerations in Omics Studies

With the exponential rise in omics-based studies (i.e., the large-scale analysis of biological molecules that underpin an organism's structure, function, and dynamics) in biomedical data science, organisations such as Encyclopedia of DNA elements (ENCODE) have established guidelines for various omics techniques. However, there is still no comprehensive consensus on best practices for experimental design in omics research, as optimal approaches depend on the specific biological question being addressed. Here, we introduce key factors that should be considered when designing an omics experiment.

1.2.1 Types of Omics Studies

A wide range of sequencing techniques is continually being developed and integrated. However, the most commonly used methods remain bulk RNA-seq, single-cell sequencing, and epigenetic sequencing-related techniques. In detail:

- **Bulk RNA-seq** [10] quantifies mature mRNA levels and is particularly useful for measuring overall gene expression across an entire tissue or population of cells.
  While it can detect mRNA isoforms and splicing patterns, it may not effectively capture transcripts that are lowly expressed, transient, or rapidly degraded.
- **Single-cell RNA sequencing (scRNA-seq)** [11] analyses gene expression at the level of individual cells, enabling researchers to study cellular heterogeneity and track lineage trajectories. This technique provides insights into cellular processes that bulk RNA-seq may overlook.
- **Epigenetic sequencing techniques** [12] examine how DNA is packaged into chromatin and how accessible it is for transcription. The DNA structure is highly dynamic, and regions of

open chromatin facilitate the binding of transcription factors (TFs), playing a critical role in gene regulation. These accessible regions account for less than 4% of the genome but contain more than 90% of TF binding sites.

Among epigenetic techniques:

- **ATAC-seq** [13] and **DNase I hypersensitive sites sequencing (DNase-seq)** [14] are complementary techniques for identifying regions of open chromatin. ATAC-seq uses Tn5 transposase to profile chromatin accessibility, while DNase-seq employs DNase I enzymatic digestion to detect nucleosome-free and nucleosome-depleted regions.
These methods enable the precise identification of regulatory genomic elements, such as promoters, enhancers, and silencers. By revealing detailed molecular insights into gene expression mechanisms, these methods help scientists understand how genes contribute to normal biological functions or diseases.
- **Chromatin immunoprecipitation sequencing** (ChIP-seq) [15] facilitates genome-wide profiling of protein–DNA interactions, allowing precise identification and characterisation of TF binding sites and their potential regulatory implications.

1.3 Key Considerations in Experimental Design for Sequencing

Experimental design in sequencing technologies represents a critical foundation for generating reliable and meaningful omics data. The success of molecular profiling techniques, such as RNA-seq, ATAC-seq, and ChIP-seq, relies on a thorough consideration of multiple experimental parameters. These parameters range from fundamental biological considerations, such as cell viability and number, to technical aspects, including sequencing depth, read length, and replicate strategies. Each decision in the experimental workflow can significantly impact data quality, resolution, and interpretability. This section explores key considerations that researchers must carefully evaluate when designing sequencing experiments. It provides insights into optimising protocols across different genomic profiling techniques to maximise scientific rigour and minimise potential sources of technical variation.

1.3.1 Cell viability

Maintaining high cell viability is essential for scRNA-seq to ensure accurate data. Excessive cell death releases RNA into the surrounding environment (ambient RNA), leading to cross-contamination between droplets and skewing results toward cell death-related pathways, which can lead to misinterpretation of data [16]. One approach to mitigating this issue is to filter samples based on their mitochondrial DNA content. High mitochondrial DNA percentages (typically >5–15%, as widely accepted across studies) are indicative of low-viability cells, as mitochondrial DNA serves as a proxy for cell death [17, 18]. However, optimal thresholds vary depending on species, sample type, and experimental conditions. They should be carefully optimised to avoid inadvertently removing viable cells of interest [19, 20]. This issue is particularly pronounced in cells with high turnover rates, such as germ cells and neutrophils, necessitating careful threshold selection [19, 21].

To minimise cell viability loss, researchers should optimise protocols at each stage of sample processing, including mechanical dissociation, activated cell sorting (FACS) and fixation, particularly when working with rare cell populations. Similarly, in ATAC-seq, low cell viability can lead to excessive chromatin fragmentation from dying cells, which oversaturates Tn5 transposase activity and compromises chromatin accessibility profiling. To prevent this, it is crucial to use fresh or well-preserved samples and perform experiments as quickly as possible to prevent sample degradation. Mechanical dissociation, FACS sorting, and fixation protocols should be carefully optimised to minimise cellular damage, especially in experiments involving rare or fragile cell populations [22].

1.3.2 Cell number

Generating enough cells for an omics experiment is a fundamental challenge. Different techniques require fewer or more cells in order to develop the required output. ATAC-seq is particularly advantageous in this regard, as it requires significantly fewer cells than its predecessors, formaldehyde-assisted isolation of regulatory elements sequencing (FAIRE-seq) and DNase-seq, which typically demand millions of cells. ATAC-seq can be performed with 25,000–75,000 cells, making it a more accessible and rapid technique. However, careful titration of cell numbers is essential to avoid over- or under-digestion, which can compromise signal-to-noise ratios and specificity [23, 22]. Conversely, ChIP-seq requires a much higher number of cells (roughly 10 million per tube) to capture sufficient binding events for Transcription factors (TFs), which are often sparsely distributed across the genome. This requirement makes ChIP-seq more challenging for studies involving rare or hard-to-grow cell types. In both bulk RNA-seq and scRNA-seq, the limited number of cells can be offset by increasing sequencing depth and using biological replicates to ensure statistical robustness.

1.3.3 Coverage and depth in sequencing

During sequencing, coverage (i.e., sequencing across the entire length of the DNA provided) and depth (i.e., the redundancy of sequencing) are considered. However, these factors play a crucial role in balancing cost against the small number of cells and few replicates, so they should be considered early in the experimental design. When cell numbers and replicates are limited, increasing sequencing depth can help compensate for these limitations. However, this comes at a higher cost, and excessive depth can increase false discovery rate (FDR),making optimisation essential.

The optimal sequencing depth is context-dependent, influenced by technological constraints and the specific research objective. Molecular representation deviates from theoretical uniformity due to inherent challenges, including sequencing artefacts, GC-content bias that disproportionately affects genomic regions with extreme nucleotide compositions, and the restricted informational content of short-read technologies ($\leq$ 250 nucleotides), which complicate the accurate distinction between genuine genetic variations and background noise. If sequencing were error-free and perfectly uniform, each RNA or DNA molecule would be proportionally represented, reducing the need for redundancy. However, errors arise from sequencing artefacts, GC-content variability, and short read lengths ($\leq$ 250 nucleotides), which make distinguishing true genetic variation from noise more challenging.

Gene expression quantification requires moderate depth, but different types of analysis demand varying depths. Highly expressed genes ($>$10 fragments per kilobase of transcript per million mapped reads (FPKM)) can be detected with $\sim$36 million mapped reads. Lowly expressed genes ($<$10 Fragments per kilobase of transcript per million mapped reads (FPKM)) require a greater depth ($\sim$80 million mapped reads) for reliable quantification. Splicing and isoform expression analysis, allele-specific expression, and single nucleotide variant (SNV) detection require even greater depth due to the need for precise sequence resolution [24].

Targeted enrichment strategies can also be used to optimise sequencing efficiency, but they come at the cost of a more targeted (and perhaps more biased) research hypothesis. For example, in RNA-seq, depletion or enrichment strategies are commonly used, such as rRNA depletion; since ribosomal RNA ($\sim$90% of total RNA) is non-informative, removing it increases the proportion of useful reads; furthermore, Poly(A) selection is another approach in bulk RNA-seq that enriches for mature mRNAs, improving transcriptome coverage [25, 26].

DNase-seq and ATAC-seq rely on high sequencing depths to comprehensively map chromatin accessibility, as the enzymatic sensitivity and chromatin structure vary significantly across genomic regions. In DNase-seq, the differential sensitivity of DNase I to DNA packaging and protein binding results in uneven cleavage patterns. In contrast, ATAC-seq's heterogeneous nature means that low accessibility regions can be easily overlooked without sufficient sequencing coverage. Consequently, both techniques require deep sequencing to ensure a representative and accurate profile of the chromatin landscape, capturing both highly accessible and more compact genomic regions. Unlike DNase-seq, which has long been the gold standard for footprinting due to its precise enzymatic cleavage, ATAC-seq footprinting is more challenging. Standard ATAC-seq requires high sequencing depths (typically 100 million uniquely aligned fragments) to less sensitively detect footprints, such as CTCF binding sites, due to the less precise insertion pattern of Tn5 transposase [27].

Omni-ATAC-seq, an improved protocol, enables footprinting analysis with shallower sequencing depths (50 million or even 25 million fragments), making it more cost-effective and improving the resolution of protein–DNA interaction detection compared to standard ATAC-seq [28]. In brief, ATAC-seq is a fast and efficient method to identify regulatory elements (such as enhancers, promoters, and boundary elements). In contrast, DNase-seq is a more challenging protocol that can reliably identify TFs (such as *CTCF* and *GATA1*) footprints [29, 30]. Standard ATAC-seq effectively detects CTCF footprints with 100 million uniquely aligned fragments.

In location-based sequencing techniques like ChIP-seq, extreme sequencing depth is not necessary, as this is essentially a targeted technique. Instead, sufficient read length and accuracy are needed to map reads precisely to the genome. However, depth requirements vary depending on the type of factor being studied: point-source factors (e.g., *REST*, a sequence-specific TF) bind to specific genomic sites and require lower sequencing depth; broad-source factors (e.g., histone modifications and RNA polymerase II) cover larger genomic regions and necessitate greater depth; mixed-source factors (e.g., RNA polymerase II) exhibit both point and broad binding characteristics, requiring an intermediate sequencing depth [31].

1.3.4 Choosing replicates over depth

In differential gene expression studies, increasing the number of biological replicates reduces the covariance of expression in low-, moderately, and highly expressed genes. In particular, for highly and moderately expressed genes, depth does not improve detection as much as biological replicates. For lowly expressed genes, however, depth can be considered as important as biological variability; however, it must be noted that depth comes at the risk of increased false-positive rates. Biological replicates also have the added benefit of capturing biological variability more effectively than extreme sequencing depth and can counter technical variability. Even when sequencing depth is limited, replicates can uncover meaningful expression trends, making them a cost-effective strategy for RNA-seq optimisation [32].

For ATAC-seq and ChIP-seq, experimental reproducibility is generally high, so studies commonly use duplicate replicates. However, increasing the number of biological replicates improves the detection of low-accessibility chromatin regions and enhances the ability to detect moderate differences in chromatin accessibility between conditions. More replicates can, however, be applied to ChIP-seq to increase the identification of differential transcription factor binding [31].

1.3.5 Read length

Even with optimal sequencing depth and coverage to minimise errors, some assembly gaps remain unresolved, particularly those caused by repetitive regions that are as long as or longer than individual reads. Paired-end sequencing helps mitigate this issue by sequencing both ends of the same DNA molecule, separated by a known distance. This approach enables the accurate placement of repetitive regions that are shorter than the fragment size; however, it cannot resolve gaps caused by longer repeats.

In bulk RNA-seq, the selection of read length and fragment size is a critical factor influencing data resolution. Single-end reads are simpler and more cost-effective, but they provide less information about transcript structure. In contrast, paired-end reads offer greater detail, enabling improved variant detection, splicing event identification, and allele-specific expression analysis. Selecting an appropriate fragment size is equally important: longer fragments improve mapping and enable better detection of splicing events, but may introduce redundancy; shorter fragments provide higher resolution but can limit the ability to detect alternative isoforms.

For ATAC-seq, the fragment size must fall within specific ranges to allow efficient tagmentation and amplification: fragments that are too large are inefficiently tagmented by Tn5 transposase, reducing library complexity; shorter fragments are preferentially amplified due to PCR biases, potentially skewing the data; larger sequencing fragments do not cluster well on flow cells, affecting sequencing efficiency. Additionally, random junction ligation biases result in ~50% of DNA fragments receiving adapters on only one end, preventing their amplification and leading to data loss.

For ChIP-seq, size selection is crucial to remove: large fragments (>450 bp), which amplify inefficiently; and small fragments (<200 bp), which may represent adapter dimers rather than meaningful chromatin fragments.

1.3.6 Batch effects

Batch effects arise from technical variations rather than biological differences and can significantly impact the interpretation of data. These effects can artificially separate similar cell populations or obscure meaningful differences, particularly in heterogeneous samples like tumours. Improper correction of batch effects may introduce additional biases. To mitigate batch effects, sequencing experiments (whether RNA-seq, ATAC-seq, or ChIP-seq) should incorporate randomisation and blocking to distribute potential biases evenly across experimental conditions. To minimise technical variability, consistent tissue storage, dissociation, and library preparation protocols should be used across each batch.

Batch effects differ by sequencing technique. Single-cell sequencing is particularly susceptible to batch effects due to variability in tissue processing and dissociation. ATAC-seq generally exhibits low batch variability because peak signals are primarily determined by chromatin accessibility rather than batch-related biases. ChIP-seq requires careful experimental design to incorporate control samples and inputs in each batch, as it is very sensitive to technical variability from library preparation steps [33].

1.4 Epigenetic Studies

ATAC-seq and ChIP-seq involve additional methodological steps, which include epigenetic modification techniques such as nuclear isolation, enzymatic reactions, and, for ChIP-seq, formaldehyde-based fixation.

1.4.1 ATAC-seq specific

Nuclei preparation stage.

Nuclei preparation in ATAC-seq should be optimised based on species, tissue type, and cellular context. Fresh samples yield the highest quality results, followed by cryopreserved, snap-frozen, and briefly cross-linked samples. Before proceeding to transposition, the integrity of the nuclei should be assessed. DAPI or Hoechst staining can confirm the intact morphology of the nuclei. Phase-contrast and fluorescence microscopy can further verify sample quality [23].

Enzymatic reaction stage.

The transposition reaction is a critical step in ATAC-seq that determines fragmentation efficiency. Insufficient transposase activity or an incorrect Tn5-to-DNA ratio results in under-tagmentation, producing large fragments ($\sim$800 bp) that hinder clustering on sequencing flow cells. Over-transposition generates excessive background noise, reducing specificity. To optimise results, the amount of nuclei and Tn5 transposase should be carefully titrated to avoid both under- and over-transposition [27].

1.4.2 ChIP-seq optimisation

Formaldehyde fixation.

Formaldehyde cross-linking requires careful optimisation to balance specificity and background noise: over-fixation (high concentration or prolonged incubation) leads to excessive non-specific binding, reducing data complexity; under-fixation results in weak or insufficient chromatin capture, leading to biased libraries [34]. Not all protein–DNA interactions are effectively preserved when formaldehyde is used alone. Certain TFs (e.g., NF-kB) require dual fixation with disuccinimidyl glutarate to enhance capture efficiency [35].

Enzymatic digestion.

Chromatin fragmentation in ChIP-seq experiments is typically performed using either enzymatic approaches, such as digestion with micrococcal nuclease, or physical methods like sonication. MNase digestion produces small, uniformly sized fragments in a laddered nucleosomal pattern, increasing resolution for histone modification studies [36]. However, it introduces bias toward AT-rich sites. Instead, sonication shears chromatin randomly via ultrasonic energy, generating unbiased fragment distributions. Regardless of the fragmentation method used, fragmentation efficiency must be assessed by running a sample on an agarose gel before proceeding with ChIP-seq [37].

Antibody incubation, chromatin washing, and elution.

Antibody selection is crucial for ChIP-seq specificity: monoclonal antibodies are preferred over polyclonal antibodies in order to minimise cross-reactivity and ensure target specificity [38].

1.4.3 Summary

Designing robust RNA-seq, ATAC-seq, and ChIP-seq experiments requires balancing multiple factors, including cell viability, sequencing depth and coverage, the number of replicates, primer selection and sequencing techniques, read lengths, and fragment size distribution. Optimisation should be done on experimental steps. While the ENCODE Consortium provides guidelines for various sequencing assays, experimental design must be tailored to the specific biological question and the size and complexity of the transcriptome being studied. Optimising these parameters can ensure higher-quality, more reproducible sequencing data that accurately reflects biological processes.

CHAPTER

2

Study Type

Biomedical studies can be broadly classified based on whether researchers actively intervene in the system being studied. The presence or absence of such intervention determines whether a study is considered *interventional* or *observational*.

Interventional studies involve an active assignment of an exposure, treatment, or intervention by the investigator. These include clinical trials, which are typically structured to test hypotheses about the efficacy or safety of a medical intervention. *Observational studies*, in contrast, do not involve active manipulation. Instead, researchers observe outcomes as they naturally occur, without influencing the assignment of treatments or exposures. These studies are essential for investigating associations, generating hypotheses, and evaluating exposures that would be unethical or impractical to randomise.

Figure 2.1 presents a flowchart classifying medical research studies. It guides researchers through a series of key design features, such as the use of control groups, randomisation, and temporal direction, to distinguish among common study types.

2.1 Observational Studies

In *observational studies*, researchers do not assign interventions or exposures; instead, they observe outcomes as they naturally occur. All *clinical decisions*, such as treatments or diagnostic testing, are determined by the standard of care rather than experimental assignment. As such, observational studies are used

10.1201/9788743812487-3

Figure 2.1: Flowchart for classifying types of medical research studies, divided into interventional studies or clinical trials (blue), and observational studies (green). Key decision points include the presence of a control group, randomisation, comparison group, and the study's temporal direction.

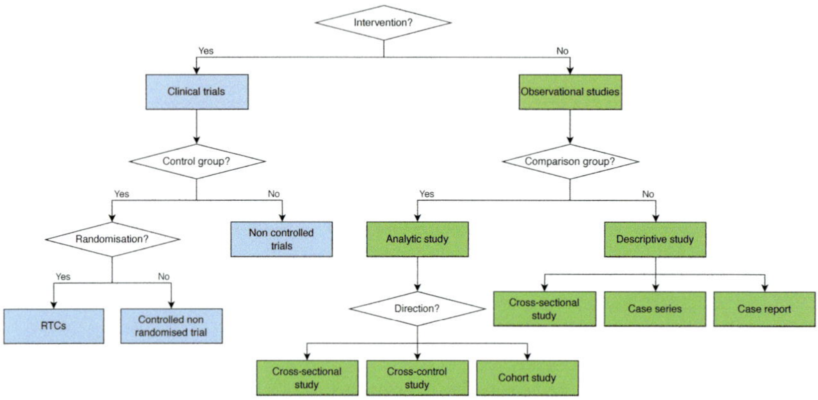

to examine associations between exposures and outcomes, but they cannot, by design, establish causality.

Observational studies can be broadly classified into:

- *Descriptive studies*, which summarise characteristics or prevalence in a population without testing specific hypotheses.
- *Analytical studies*, which aim to identify potential associations between exposures and outcomes.

Descriptive designs include case reports and case series, while analytical designs encompass cross-sectional, cohort, case-control, and nested case-control studies. In this chapter, we focus on *analytical observational studies*, which are frequently used in biomedical research to evaluate risk factors, diagnostic accuracy, and disease progression.

2.1.1 Cross-sectional studies

Cross-sectional studies (CSSs) analyse data collected from a population at a single point in time. Data are typically gathered from databases, surveys, questionnaires, interviews, or electronic health records. Cross-sectional study (CSS)s are used to:

- Measure *disease prevalence* or health indicators in a population.
- Investigate *risk factors* by comparing exposures between groups (e.g., smokers vs. non-smokers).
- Evaluate *diagnostic performance* against a gold standard.
- Assess the *efficacy* of an intervention retrospectively.

Cross-sectional designs may serve both descriptive and analytical purposes. While descriptive CSSs estimate the prevalence of outcomes, analytical CSSs examine the associations between exposures and outcomes at a single time point. Inclusion criteria must be carefully designed to avoid selection bias and ensure generalisability.

Example:

Bień *et al.* (2025) conducted a cross-sectional study evaluating the prevalence of severe psoriasis (descriptive aim) and its association with major life-changing decisions (analytical aim) [39].

2.1.2 Cohort studies

Cohort studies are longitudinal designs in which individuals with and without a given exposure are followed over time to assess the incidence of specific outcomes. These are typically *prospective* in nature, meaning data are collected going forward from the point of exposure. However, retrospective cohort studies are also possible using historical records. Cohort designs are ideal for:

- Estimating *risk ratios* and *incidence rates* .
- Studying the *natural history* of diseases.
- Assessing *temporal relationships* between exposures and outcomes.

Their main limitations are logistical: they often require large sample sizes and long follow-up periods, particularly for diseases with long latency periods, such as cancer.

Example:

In a prospective cohort study, Conte *et al.* (2024) followed 90,119 women from 1990 to 2018 to evaluate whether MALTectomy was associated with increased psoriasis risk. Incidence was quantified using the hazard ratio (HR) [40].

2.1.3 Case-control studies

Case-control studies (CCSs) begin by identifying individuals with the outcome of interest (cases) and those without it (controls). Investigators then retrospectively assess whether subjects were exposed to a potential risk factor. These studies are efficient for investigating rare diseases or outcomes with long latency periods. Case-control study (CCS)s are particularly suited for:

- Studying *rare conditions* (e.g., adverse drug reactions).
- Evaluating *multiple exposures* for a single outcome.
- Conducting preliminary investigations where cohort studies are impractical.

However, CCSs cannot estimate disease prevalence or incidence, and they are prone to recall and selection bias.

Example:

Shahin *et al.* (2025) conducted a case-control study comparing patients with and without atopic dermatitis. Oral health and microbiome profiles were evaluated using 16S rRNA sequencing to explore microbial differences associated with the condition [41].

2.1.4 Nested case-control studies

Nested case-control studies are a subtype of case-control studies conducted within a well-defined cohort. After establishing a cohort and observing outcomes over time, a subset of cases and matched controls is selected for additional analysis. This design is especially useful when biomarker assays or imaging are expensive or when detailed data collection is only feasible in a subsample. Some advantages are:

- Reduced cost and effort relative to full-cohort analysis.
- Improved validity due to the initial cohort's prospective nature.
- Flexibility in retrospective biomarker or genomic testing.

Example:

Vela *et al.* (2021) used a nested case-control design within the DANBIO registry. Among patients with psoriatic arthritis, those who had died were compared to surviving controls to investigate whether pain scores were associated with all-cause mortality using 100 mm VAS assessments [42].

2.2 Interventional Studies and Clinical Trials

Interventional studies are those in which researchers actively assign exposures or treatments to study participants, typically to test the efficacy or safety of a therapeutic intervention. These studies may include or exclude control groups and may be randomised or non-randomised depending on the study design.

2.2.1 Randomised controlled trials

Randomised control trials (RCTs) are considered the gold standard for evaluating the efficacy of medical interventions. In an RCT, participants are randomly assigned to one of two or more groups: an *experimental group* receiving the treatment, and a *control group* receiving a placebo, standard care, or an alternative treatment. Both groups are then followed over a pre-specified period, during which outcomes are assessed according to the study protocol. Because randomisation aims to make the groups statistically equivalent in terms of both known and unknown factors, differences in outcomes can, in principle, be attributed to the treatment itself.

Different RCT designs are used depending on the hypothesis and logistical constraints (see Figure 2.2).

- **Parallel design:** Each group receives a different treatment throughout the study.
- **Crossover design:** Participants receive multiple treatments in sequence, separated by a washout period. To be more precise, the recruited subjects experience all types of treatment in different periods. During the first period, one group receives intervention A and one group receives intervention B; then, the treatments are reversed.

- **N-of-1 trials:** Each patient serves as their own control, receiving alternating treatments in repeated cycles.

Figure 2.2: Schematic representation of different RCT study designs: N-of-1 (top), crossover (middle), and parallel (bottom) arrangements of treatments A and B.

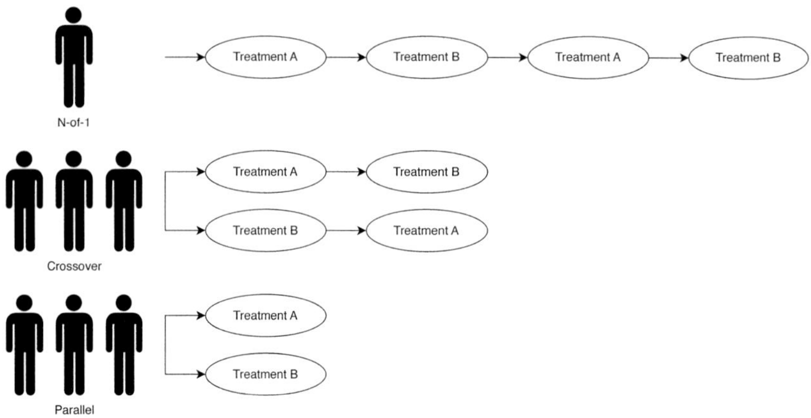

RCTs may be designed to assess:

- **Superiority:** Whether a new treatment is better than the current standard.
- **Non-inferiority:** Whether a new treatment is not worse than the standard by more than a predefined margin.
- **Equivalence:** Whether two treatments have no clinically meaningful difference.

Blinding and control:

To reduce bias, blinding may be applied at different levels:

- **Single-blind:** The patient is unaware of the treatment group.
- **Double-blind:** Both patient and clinician are unaware.
- **Triple-blind:** Patient, clinician, and data analyst are all blinded.

Use of *placebo* and attention to *nocebo* effects (negative outcomes arising from expectations) are critical in trial design.

Omics and biomarker integration:

Modern trials increasingly integrate *omics data*, such as genomics, proteomics, or metabolomics, either as primary/secondary outcomes or to define inclusion criteria. While this allows for improved stratification and reduced biological variability, it can limit external validity and generalisability to broader populations. Indeed, RCTs allow for cleanly and controllably recovering causal effects, unlike observational studies, where confounding can obscure treatment effects. They are essential for hypothesis-driven, prospective evaluation of treatment effects and are the cornerstone of evidence-based medicine. However, they are expensive and time-consuming and may not reflect real-world clinical conditions due to narrow inclusion criteria and short follow-up durations.

2.2.2 Phases of clinical trials in drug development

Clinical drug development is traditionally divided into four distinct phases, each with specific objectives:

2.2.2.1 Phase 1: Safety and tolerability

The primary goal of Phase 1 trials is to evaluate safety, dose tolerance, and pharmacokinetics in a small group of healthy volunteers. Multiple dose levels are tested to identify the maximum tolerated dose and common adverse events.

Example:

Kato *et al.* (2024) conducted a double-blind, placebo-controlled, single and multiple ascending dose Phase 1 study evaluating ME3183, an oral PDE4 inhibitor, in 126 healthy participants. Safety, tolerability, and pharmacokinetics were assessed [43].

2.2.2.2 Phase 2: Efficacy and dose ranging

In Phase 2, the therapeutic effect of the drug is assessed in patients with the target disease. Participants are typically randomised across different dose arms, and placebo controls may be included where ethical considerations permit.

Example:

Catlett *et al.* (2024) ran a randomised, double-blind, placebo-controlled Phase 2 trial evaluating deucravacitinib, a selective TYK2 inhibitor, in psoriatic patients. Multiple-dose regimens were tested, and pharmacodynamic responses were assessed using proteomic and cytokine-based biomarkers [44].

2.2.2.3 Phase 3: Efficacy and safety in large populations

Phase 3 trials confirm efficacy and monitor adverse events in large, diverse patient populations. These trials compare the new intervention to existing standards of care, providing data for regulatory approval.

Example:

Papp *et al.* (2023) conducted a multicentre, randomised, double-blind, superiority Phase 3 trial comparing mirikizumab, a novel IL-23p19 inhibitor, to secukinumab in patients with moderate-to-severe psoriasis [45].

2.2.2.4 Phase 4: Post-Marketing Surveillance

These studies are conducted after regulatory approval to monitor the long-term safety and efficacy of the product in real-world use. They aim to detect rare adverse events and evaluate broader health outcomes such as quality of life.

Example:

Bhatia *et al.* (2024) performed a Phase 4 study evaluating long-term health-related quality of life in patients treated with tildrakizumab for moderate-to-severe psoriasis over 64 weeks [46].

Part II

Statistical Methods and Machine Learning Techniques: From Hypothesis Testing to Predictive Modelling

CHAPTER

3

Statistical Analysis in Biomedical Research

Statistical inference is a probabilistic framework for drawing conclusions about unknown population characteristics or underlying mechanisms using observed data, while quantifying the uncertainty associated with those conclusions. In biomedical data science, inference helps quantify uncertainty, test hypotheses, and guide evidence-based decision-making. Rather than providing absolute answers, statistical models estimate how confident we can be about observed patterns and whether these patterns are likely to generalise to the broader population.

This chapter presents key statistical concepts and tools essential for analysing biomedical data and performing inference on their underlying distributions. It includes Python code snippets, primarily using the scipy library, to provide hands-on examples.

3.1 Descriptive and Inferential Foundations

3.1.1 Point estimates, confidence intervals, and odds ratio

A *point estimate* provides a scalar approximation of an unknown *parameter* of the population distribution, for instance, the sample mean or an odds ratio (OR) [47]. Since point estimates are subject to sampling variability, they rarely match the true population value. Because point estimates are based on a finite sample, they vary across samples and are unlikely to represent the actual population

10.1201/9788743812487-5

parameter accurately. The *standard error (SE)* quantifies this sampling variability: it measures how much an estimate is expected to fluctuate if its computation were repeated many times under the same conditions. For the sample mean (under certain assumptions on how the data collection process), the Standard error (SE) is calculated as the sample standard deviation (SD) s divided by the square root of the sample size n:

$$SE = \frac{s}{\sqrt{n}}$$

More generally, each estimator (e.g., a proportion, regression coefficient, or Odds ratio (OR)) has its own formula for the SE, reflecting the fact that sampling is a function of both the model and the data.

A *confidence interval (CI)* offers a range of values with a chosen degree of plausibility for an unknown parameter, capturing the uncertainty inherent in a sample-based estimate and relying on the underlying sampling distribution [48]. For example, a 95% Confidence interval (CI) indicates that if the same experiment were repeated multiple times, and a new interval were computed for each sample, around 95% of the resulting intervals would include the true value of the parameter. However, this does not imply a 95% probability that the specific interval obtained from one dataset contains the true value—rather, the interval either does or does not include it. The 95% refers to the *long-run frequency* of intervals covering the truth across repeated samples. Thus, the interpretation pertains to the procedure, not to the specific interval. CIs are commonly constructed as the point estimate $\pm$ a multiple of its SE, linking them directly to measures of sampling variability.

CIs are particularly useful in biomedical research because they reflect both the estimate and the uncertainty, providing more insight than a simple *p-value* [49]. For example, a narrow interval suggests precise estimation, while a wide interval highlights uncertainty. In addition, CIs help assess *clinical relevance*, not just statistical significance. While a p-value only indicates whether an effect is or is not likely to be a result of chance, a CI represents the range of effect sizes compatible with the data. By examining whether this range includes values considered clinically meaningful, researchers can determine whether a statistically significant result is also clinically important in practice. Nonetheless, CIs are closely related to *hypothesis tests* (and hence p-values). The former will be introduced in Section 3.1.2.

An *OR* is a statistical metric which expresses the degree of association between two events, such as an exposure and a corresponding outcome [47]. It is defined as the ratio between the odds of the event happening in the treated group and the odds of the event happening in the non-treated group.

$$\mathrm{OR} = \frac{\text{odds in exposed}}{\text{odds in non-exposed}}, \quad \text{where odds} = \frac{\text{probability of event}}{1 - \text{probability of event}}.$$

An OR of 1 indicates no association as the odds do not change across the groups. An OR greater than 1 indicates evidence of treatment being associated with increased odds of the outcome, whereas an OR less than 1 indicates decreased odds. It is essential to report the OR alongside its 95% CI, as it reflects the estimate's precision. Importantly, suppose the CI spans the value 1. In that case, the result is not statistically significant at the 5% level, meaning that a two-sided hypothesis test at this significance level would fail to reject the null hypothesis that the OR is equal to 1. In the biomedical field, ORs are frequently employed in case-control studies to evaluate the potential association between a specific exposure and a given outcome.

Example:

As an example, consider an experimental study investigating the association between aspirin intake and the risk of ischemic stroke among women. The corresponding data are organised in the following contingency table:

	Ischemic stroke	No stroke
Aspirin group	176	21,035
Placebo group	230	21,018

The objective is to determine whether aspirin usage lowers the risk of ischemic stroke. To compute the OR and its 95% CI in Python, we use the odds_ratio function from the scipy.stats.contingency module.

```
from scipy.stats.contingency import odds_ratio

res = odds_ratio([[177, 231], [21036, 21019]])
```

The full executable code corresponding to this example is available online and can be accessed, reused, and commented on at: https://github.com/RiverPublishers/Computational-Approaches-in-Biology-and-Medicine/blob/main/Chapter3.ipynb

Here are a few points for explanation and interpretation:

- OR: the computed value indicates the odds of experiencing an ischemic stroke in the aspirin group relative to the placebo group.

- A 95% CI suggests that, in repeated sampling, 95% of such intervals would be expected to include the real OR.
- If the entire CI is below 1, it suggests that aspirin usage is associated with a statistically significant mitigation of the risk of ischemic stroke.

3.1.2 Hypothesis testing and p-value

Hypothesis testing is a fundamental aspect of statistical inference. It offers a formal framework for evaluating whether the evidence in the observed data is strong enough to reject a null hypothesis (H_0) in support of an alternative hypothesis (H_1). In the context of biomedical research, hypothesis testing is crucial for informing decisions, such as determining whether a new treatment yields better outcomes than a control. The standard procedure typically involves the following steps:

1. **Formulate the null and alternative hypotheses.** In the context of biomedical research, the null hypothesis (H_0) is often that no effect or difference exists between groups, while the alternative hypothesis (H_1) is that a real effect or difference does exist.
2. **Select an appropriate statistical test** based on the study design, data type, and assumptions (e.g., independence, normality, equal variances). The choice should align with the research question and hypotheses.
3. **Compute the test statistic** $\hat{t}$ from the sample data using the formula specific to the chosen test. Under the null hypothesis H_0, this statistic follows a known theoretical sampling distribution.
4. **Calculate the p-value**, defined as the probability under H_0 of observing a value of the test statistic as or more extreme than the one actually obtained in the sample [49], i.e.

$$p = \mathbb{P}(t \text{ as or more extreme than } \hat{t} \mid H_0)$$

5. **Make a decision** by comparing the p-value to the chosen significance level α (typically 0.05). If $p < \alpha$, reject H_0; otherwise, fail to reject H_0. Interpret this result in context, considering the estimated effect size and its CI, rather than relying solely on the p-value.

A small p-value (typically less than 0.05) indicates that the observed data would be highly improbable if the null hypothesis were true, thereby offering evidence against H_0. However, the p-value *is not* the probability that the null hypothesis is correct, nor does it convey the magnitude or clinical significance of the observed effect. Common misinterpretations of the p-value are [50]:

- The p-value is the probability that H_0 is true.
- The p-value is the chance of the results occurring due to random error alone (i.e., the probability of making an error).

- A statistically significant result ($p < 0.05$) implies clinical significance.

Example:

A p-value of 0.04 suggests that, under the null hypothesis, there would be a 4% probability of observing the current data (or more extreme) purely due to chance. For instance, suppose a researcher is testing a new drug. If the p-value is 0.04, and α is 0.05, the researcher rejects H_0, concluding there is statistically significant evidence that the drug differs from the control.

It is worth noting that, in clinical research, it is essential to complement p-values with effect sizes and CIs to determine whether an effect is both statistically and clinically meaningful. Effect sizes, which measure the magnitude of differences or associations, should also be reported. Additionally, graphical summaries should be provided to offer visual insight into the data and support interpretation. Using p-values in conjunction with other inferential tools ensures the results are not only *statistically significant* but also *scientifically and clinically meaningful*.

3.1.3 Type I and type II errors

When performing hypothesis tests, two types of errors can occur [51, 52]:

- **Type I error** (whose probability we call α): Rejecting H_0 when it is true (false positive).
- **Type II error** (whose probability we call β): Failing to reject H_0 when H_1 is true (false negative).

Note that the significance level α is equivalent to the probability of a Type I error, as it is exactly the probability of rejecting the null hypothesis under the null hypothesis, i.e. when it is actually true. Hence, when constructing the test, it is possible to explicitly choose the probability of such an error.

Unlike α, which is chosen, β cannot be computed, as it depends on the true distribution under the alternative hypothesis, which is unknown in practice. The *power* of a statistical test refers to the likelihood of rejecting the null hypothesis when the alternative hypothesis is indeed correct [51]. It is defined as:

$$\text{Power} = 1 - \beta.$$

Several factors, including effect size, sample size, data variability, and the selected significance threshold, influence power. Lowering the significance level imposes a stricter criterion for rejecting the null hypothesis, which in turn raises the risk of a Type II error and hinders statistical power. Biomedical studies often aim for a power of 80% or more to ensure adequate sensitivity for detecting clinically relevant effects. Low power increases the risk of missing real effects (false negatives), while a low α (e.g., 0.01) reduces false positives but may require larger sample sizes.

3.1.4 One-tailed vs. two-tailed tests

One-tailed tests are used when the research hypothesis specifies a particular direction of effect (e.g., a new treatment is expected to improve outcomes compared with control) [53, 54]. *Two-tailed tests*, by contrast, are applied when any deviation from the null hypothesis is of interest, whether the treatment performs better or worse than the control. Because the significance level α is divided between both tails of the sampling distribution, two-tailed tests are more conservative, that is, they require stronger evidence to reject the null hypothesis in a given direction. In biomedical research, two-tailed tests are generally preferred unless existing knowledge strongly justifies expecting an effect only in a certain direction.

3.2 Parametric Tests (Mean-based)

Parametric tests are statistical procedures which depend on assumptions regarding the characteristics of the data-generating process, commonly including normality of the data, homogeneity of variance, and independence of observations [55]. When these assumptions are reasonably met, parametric tests are highly efficient and statistically powerful, providing reliable estimates of group means and differences between them. In biomedical research, parametric tests are widely used to compare means across one, two, or multiple groups, under the assumption of homoscedasticity (equal variances) and interval-scale measurements. This section introduces the most common parametric tests for hypothesis testing involving means, including one-sample, two-sample, and analysis of variance (ANOVA) tests for comparing three or more groups [56].

3.2.1 One-sample analysis

A one-sample test is used when comparing the mean of a unique sample to a known or hypothesised reference value. This often occurs in biomedical applications, for instance, to determine whether the mean cholesterol level in a sample exceeds a clinical threshold. The null hypothesis H_0 posits that the true population mean equals the reference value μ_0. The test statistic is calculated as:

$$t = \frac{\bar{x} - \mu_0}{s/\sqrt{n}}$$

where $\bar{x}$ is the sample mean, s the sample Standard deviation (SD), and n sample size. The observed test statistic is then contrasted to the t-distribution with $n-1$ degrees of freedom (df) to determine whether there is statistical significance.

In Python, we can do this analysis as follows. First, we sample from some random variables using a fixed seed, ensuring that each run yields the same results for comparison. In this case, we produce a sample from the Student t-distribution:

```
import numpy as np
import scipy.stats as stats

np.random.seed(42)

x = stats.t.rvs(10, size=1000)
```

The full executable code corresponding to this example is available online and can be accessed, reused, and commented on at: https://github.com/RiverPublishers/Computational-Approaches-in-Biology-and-Medicine/blob/main/Chapter3.ipynb

In this example, the t-distribution has 10 Degrees of freedom (df), and the sample size is 1000. The parameters loc and scale are left to their default values (i.e., zero and one, respectively), while x will be a numpy array with 1000 sample elements.

3.2.1.1 t-distribution and z-distribution

The decision to use the *t-distribution* or the *z-distribution* (i.e., *the standard normal distribution*) in hypothesis testing or CI construction depends on sample size and on whether the population SD is known.

- The *z-distribution* is applied when the population SD is known, or the sample size is sufficiently large.
- *t-distribution* is employed when the population SD is unknown and has to be estimated from the data, especially in small samples. As the sample size grows, the t-distribution converges to the standard normal distribution.

The t-distribution represents the standardised distance between the sample mean and the population mean when the true SD is unknown, assuming that the data are drawn from a normally distributed population. It is computed using the sample SD and has the following characteristics:

- Similar to the z-distribution, the *t-distribution* has a continuous and smooth shape.
- It is symmetric around zero, like the *z-distribution*.
- The *t-distribution* is parametrised by the *df*, which is generally set to be the sample size minus one.

The code below illustrates the z-distribution alongside several t-distributions with varying df. As the df increase, the t-distribution converges toward the z-distribution, exhibiting progressively thinner tails.

```
import numpy as np
import matplotlib.pyplot as plt
from scipy.stats import norm, t

np.random.seed(42)

# Set publication-style aesthetics
sns.set_theme(style="whitegrid", context="talk")

# Define the range for x (covering the tails of the
↪  distributions)
x = np.linspace(-5, 5, 500)

# Calculate the PDF for the standard normal distribution
y_normal = norm.pdf(x, loc=0, scale=1)

# Calculate the PDFs for t-distributions with different
↪  degrees of freedom
y_t1 = t.pdf(x, df=1)
y_t2 = t.pdf(x, df=2)
y_t10 = t.pdf(x, df=10)

colours = sns.color_palette("dark", n_colors=4)

# Plot all distributions
plt.figure(figsize=(10, 6))
plt.plot(x, y_normal, label='Standard Normal ($\mu=0$,
↪  $\sigma=1$)', color=colours[0], linewidth=1)
```

```
plt.plot(x, y_t1, label='t-distribution (df=1)',
 ↪ color=colours[1], linestyle='--', linewidth=1)
plt.plot(x, y_t2, label='t-distribution (df=2)',
 ↪ color=colours[2], linestyle='-.', linewidth=1)
plt.plot(x, y_t10, label='t-distribution (df=10)',
 ↪ color=colours[3], linestyle=':', linewidth=1)

# Add title, labels, grid, and legend
plt.xlabel('x', fontsize=16)
plt.ylabel('Probability Density', fontsize=16)
plt.title('Standard Normal vs t-Distributions',
 ↪ fontsize=20, fontweight='bold')
plt.legend(frameon=True, fontsize=14)
plt.grid(True, linestyle='--', alpha=0.6)
sns.despine()

# Show the plot
plt.tight_layout()
plt.show()
```

The full executable code corresponding to this example is available online and can be accessed, reused, and commented on at: https://github.com/RiverPublishers/Computational-Approaches-in-Biology-and-Medicine/blob/main/Chapter3.ipynb

Figure 3.1: Comparison of three t-distributions and a z-distribution.

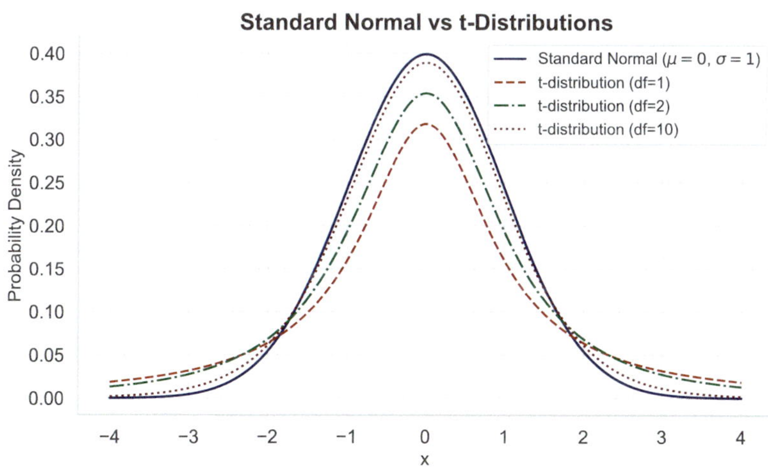

3.2.1.2 One-sample t-test

A *t-test* (also referred to as *Student's t-test*) is a statistical test employed to compare the means of two populations [55]. Depending on the study design, different types of t-tests are used: a *one-sample t-test* evaluates whether the mean of a single group significantly differs from a reference value; an *independent two-sample t-test* assesses whether two unrelated groups have different means; and a *paired t-test* (or *dependent samples t-test*) tests for differences between matched or repeated measurements on the same subjects.

The first step in conducting a t-test involves choosing the null and alternative hypotheses, as well as selecting an acceptable level of risk for making an incorrect inference. For instance, when comparing two group means, the null hypothesis (H_0) might state that no difference exists between the two groups. We then choose a *significance level* (α), which defines the probability of wrongly rejecting H_0 when it holds.

Subsequently, we compute a *test statistic* based on the sample data and compare it to a critical value derived from the *t-distribution*. If the observed test statistic falls in the rejection region, we reject the null hypothesis; otherwise, we fail to reject it.

Although *t-tests* are generally robust to moderate violations of their underlying assumptions, their validity still relies on several key conditions:

- The data should be continuous (i.e. made of real numbers).
- The observations must be drawn randomly from the target population.
- The considered groups should exhibit *homogeneity of variance*, meaning their variability is roughly equal.
- The data should follow an approximately normal distribution, or the sample size should be sufficiently large (typically $n > 30$), as either condition supports the assumption of a normal sampling distribution for the sample mean.

In our one-sample analysis, we employ the t-test to determine if the sample mean differs significantly from a theoretical expectation. We first compute the theoretical expectation. In our setting, the population distribution follows a t-distribution with 10 df. This makes the t-test appropriate, as the t-distribution with 10 df closely approximates the standard normal distribution, thus satisfying a key assumption of the t-test.

```
m, v, s, k = stats.t.stats(11, moments='mvsk')
```

The full executable code corresponding to this example is available online and can be accessed, reused, and commented on at: https://github.com/RiverPublishers/Computational-Approaches-in-Biology-and-Medicine/blob/main/Chapter3.ipynb

Here, m, v, s, and k represent the theoretical expectation, variance, skewness, and kurtosis of the distribution, respectively.

```
print('t-statistic = %5.2f pvalue = %5.3f'
 ↪  %(stats.ttest_1samp(x, m)))
```

The full executable code corresponding to this example is available online and can be accessed, reused, and commented on at: https://github.com/RiverPublishers/Computational-Approaches-in-Biology-and-Medicine/blob/main/Chapter3.ipynb

This gives a t-statistic of 0.39 and a p-value of 0.696. With an α of 10%, we fail to reject the hypothesis that the sample mean equals zero (i.e., the m previously computed).

We provide an additional example, this time with a sample obtained from a normal distribution with a mean of 20 and a SD of 1.

```
import numpy as np
import scipy.stats as stats
from scipy.stats import norm

np.random.seed(42)

x = norm.rvs(loc=20, scale=1, size=1000)
mvsk = norm(loc=20, scale=1).stats(moments='mvsk')
print('t-statistic = %5.2f pvalue = %6.3f'
 ↪  %stats.ttest_1samp(x, mvsk[0]))
```

The full executable code corresponding to this example is available online and can be accessed, reused, and commented on at: https://github.com/RiverPublishers/Computational-Approaches-in-Biology-and-Medicine/blob/main/Chapter3.ipynb

This yields a t-statistic of -0.62 and a p-value of 0.536. At an α error of 10%, we cannot reject the hypothesis that the sample mean is equal to 20.

3.2.2 Two-sample analysis

In many real-world scenarios, researchers and analysts seek to compare two groups to ascertain whether a significant difference exists between them. This comparison can range from evaluating the effectiveness of two different treatments to assessing changes in performance before and after an intervention. Two-sample analysis provides a statistical framework for rigorously addressing such questions.

We start by introducing two foundational methods for comparing the means of two groups: the independent two-sample t-test and the paired t-test. While both tests evaluate differences between two means, they are appropriate in distinct contexts. We must distinguish between *independent* and *paired* samples. In *independent samples*, the two groups consist of different individuals (e.g., treatment vs. control). The test compares the means of the two independent groups. In *paired samples*, the same subjects are measured before and after an intervention, or matched pairs (e.g., twin studies). The test evaluates the mean difference within pairs. Thus, the paired t-test is used when the samples are dependent or matched in some way, while the independent two-sample t-test is used when the two groups are unrelated.

3.2.2.1 The independent two-sample t-test

The *independent samples t-test* (also called the *two-sample t-test*) is employed to evaluate whether the means of two distinct populations differ significantly. This test is appropriate when the data points are independent, drawn randomly from two normally distributed populations, and when the two groups being compared exhibit equal variances.

To ascertain whether the means of two groups differ, we compute a test statistic and contrast it with a critical value from the *t-distribution*. Again, this process involves four fundamental steps:

1. Choose the acceptable level of risk for making a Type I error; this is the significance level, α, which defines the threshold for declaring a statistically significant difference.
2. We calculate a test statistic. Under different SEs in the two samples, we have:

$$t = \frac{\bar{X}_1 - \bar{X}_2}{\sqrt{\frac{s_1^2}{n_1} + \frac{s_2^2}{n_2}}}. \tag{3.1}$$

In the case of equal SE, the formula changes into:

$$t = \frac{\bar{X}_1 - \bar{X}_2}{s_p\sqrt{\frac{1}{n_1} + \frac{1}{n_2}}}, \tag{3.2}$$

and the pooled variance formula is:

$$s_p^2 = \frac{(n_1 - 1)s_1^2 + (n_2 - 1)s_2^2}{n_1 + n_2 - 2}. \tag{3.3}$$

3. Determine the critical value from the *t-distribution* under the null hypothesis, which states the two group means are equal. This requires the significance level α from step 1 and the appropriate df, calculated as $n_1 + n_2 - 2$.

These two t-scores can be easily implemented in Python using the SciPy library. Let's start by generating two independent samples from two identical normal distributions. This implies the same mean and SD, resulting in a t-score of -0.403 and a p-value of 0.687.

```
import numpy as np
import scipy.stats as stats

np.random.seed(42)

rvs1 = stats.norm.rvs(loc=6, scale=11, size=500)
rvs2 = stats.norm.rvs(loc=6, scale=11, size=500)
stats.ttest_ind(rvs1, rvs2, equal_var=True)
```

The full executable code corresponding to this example is available online and can be accessed, reused, and commented on at: https://github.com/RiverPublishers/Computational-Approaches-in-Biology-and-Medicine/blob/main/Chapter3.ipynb

This result implies that we cannot reject the null hypothesis of equal means in the samples. On the other hand, we could try out with a different sample from a normally distributed population with equal variance but a different mean. In this case, the p-value would be small enough to reject the null hypothesis.

```
import numpy as np
import scipy.stats as stats

np.random.seed(42)
```

```
rvs1 = stats.norm.rvs(loc=6, scale=11, size=500)
rvs3 = stats.norm.rvs(loc=9, scale=11, size=500)
stats.ttest_ind(rvs1, rvs3, equal_var=True)
```

The full executable code corresponding to this example is available online and can be accessed, reused, and commented on at: https://github.com/RiverPublishers/Computational-Approaches-in-Biology-and-Medicine/blob/main/Chapter3.ipynb

Indeed, the p-value for the t-score is 1.783×10^{-6}.

If the variances between groups are unequal, we can apply Welch's t-test, which adjusts the df accordingly and does not assume equal variances.

```
import numpy as np
import scipy.stats as stats

np.random.seed(42)

rvs1 = stats.norm.rvs(loc=6, scale=11, size=500)
rvs4 = stats.norm.rvs(loc=6, scale=6, size=500)
stats.ttest_ind(rvs1, rvs4, equal_var=False)
```

The full executable code corresponding to this example is available online and can be accessed, reused, and commented on at: https://github.com/RiverPublishers/Computational-Approaches-in-Biology-and-Medicine/blob/main/Chapter3.ipynb

Here, the p-value of the score is 0.833, making rejection of the null hypothesis non-feasible.

3.2.2.2 Paired t-test

The *paired t-test* is a statistical test with the objective of assessing whether the average difference between paired observations is significantly different from zero. This test is appropriate when each data point consists of two related measurements—for instance, pre- and post-treatment values from the same individual. A key assumption is that the distribution of the differences between paired values is approximately normal. Specifically, the following conditions must be met:

- The subjects are independent; the measurements from one individual do not influence those of another.
- Each pair of observations must come from the same subject (e.g., before-and-after weight for the same smoker).
- The distribution of the paired differences is approximately normal.

The test statistic (t-score) is calculated as the mean of the paired differences divided by the SE of those differences. This value is then compared against the critical value from the *t-distribution*, using a significance level α defined *a priori* and df equal to $n - 1$, where n is the number of pairs.

The null hypothesis for the paired t-test states that the mean difference between the paired measurements is zero.

The following code snippet provides an example of a paired t-test in Python with synthetic data from a normally distributed population.

```
import numpy as np
import scipy.stats as stats

np.random.seed(42)

# Sample data: Before and After measurements (Paired
 ↪  samples)
before = np.random.normal(loc=110, scale=12, size=30)
after  = before + np.random.normal(loc=-2, scale=5,
 ↪  size=30)

# Perform paired t-test
t_stat, p_value = stats.ttest_rel(before, after)

# Print results
print(f"Paired t-test statistic: {t_stat:.4f}, pvalue:
 ↪  {p_value:.4f}")
```

The full executable code corresponding to this example is available online and can be accessed, reused, and commented on at: https://github.com/RiverPublishers/Computational-Approaches-in-Biology-and-Medicine/blob/main/Chapter3.ipynb

3.2.3 Multi-group analysis

When comparing more than two groups, traditional two-sample methods fall short. Relying on repeated t-tests not only increases the probability of a Type I error but also fails to provide a unified framework for evaluating group differences. Indeed, when testing multiple hypotheses (e.g., thousands of genes or biomarkers), the likelihood of obtaining at least one false positive increases. Thus, when comparing multiple groups, we can use a multiple comparison method.

3.2.3.1 One-way ANOVA

To compare means across multiple groups, statisticians employ *analysis of variance (ANOVA)* [56], a technique for assessing whether the means of three or more independent groups differ significantly. The term *one-way* refers to the fact that the analysis involves a single categorical independent variable (or *factor*) used to define the groups. The objective is to determine whether the various levels of this factor have a measurable effect on a continuous dependent variable. ANOVA achieves this by decomposing the total variability in the data into portions attributable to variation *between* and *within* groups. This allows for a global test of significance across all groups simultaneously. For the results of one-way ANOVA to be valid, the following assumptions have to hold:

- Observations must be independent; the measurement from one subject does not influence that of another.
- Each group must be drawn from a population via random sampling.
- The data within each group should be normally distributed.
- The dependent variable must be continuous.
- The variance of all groups should be the same (homogeneity of variance).

More formally, one-way ANOVA is used to test the null hypothesis (H_0) that groups have all the same mean against the alternative hypothesis (H_1) that at least one of them differs in mean from the others.

As an example, consider a manufacturing process in which you want to assess whether different production lots, operators, or material batches affect product quality. You might test this by running the process at three or more levels of the factor of interest and collecting random samples from each run. If ANOVA indicates statistically significant differences among the group means (under sound experimental conditions), this provides evidence that the factor in question has an impact on the outcome.

To compute the one-way ANOVA, we follow this procedure:

1. The total sum of squares (SST) measures the total variation in the dataset and is computed as:

$$SST = \sum_{i=1}^{N} (X_i - \bar{X})^2, \tag{3.4}$$

where:

- X_i are individual observations.
- $\bar{X}$ is the *grand mean* (mean of all observations).
- N is the total number of observations.

2. The between-group sum of squares (SSB) quantifies the variability **between** the group means:

$$SSB = \sum_{j=1}^{k} n_j (\bar{X}_j - \bar{X})^2, \tag{3.5}$$

where k is the number of groups, n_j is the number of observations in group j, $\bar{X}_j$ is the mean of group j, and $\bar{X}$ is the grand mean.

3. The within-group sum of squares (SSW) quantifies the variability *within* each group:

$$SSW = \sum_{j=1}^{k} \sum_{i=1}^{n_j} (X_{ij} - \bar{X}_j)^2, \tag{3.6}$$

where:

- X_{ij} is an individual observation in group j.
- $\bar{X}_j$ is the mean of group j.

4. The total sum of squares is the sum of between-group and within-group sums of squares:

$$SST = SSB + SSW. \tag{3.7}$$

5. The F-statistic for one-way ANOVA is computed as:

$$F = \frac{\text{MSB}}{\text{MSW}} \tag{3.8}$$

where:

- $MSB = \frac{SSB}{k-1}$ is the *mean square between groups*.
- $MSW = \frac{SSW}{N-k}$ is the *mean square within groups*.
- $k - 1$ and $N - k$ are the df for the numerator and denominator, respectively.

6. The F-statistic follows an $F(k-1, N-k)$ distribution.

We now provide a simple example of one-way ANOVA in Python:

```
import numpy as np
import scipy.stats as stats

np.random.seed(42)

# Example data: Three groups with different means
group1 = np.array([5, 6, 8, 7, 6])
group2 = np.array([10, 12, 11, 9, 13])
group3 = np.array([15, 17, 16, 14, 18])

# Combine groups into a single dataset
data = np.concatenate([group1, group2, group3])
group_labels = ['G1'] * len(group1) + ['G2'] *
↪ len(group2) + ['G3'] * len(group3)

# Compute grand mean
grand_mean = np.mean(data)

# Compute SSB (Between-group sum of squares)
ssb = sum(len(g) * (np.mean(g) - grand_mean) ** 2 for g
↪ in [group1, group2, group3])

# Compute SSW (Within-group sum of squares)
ssw = sum(np.sum((g - np.mean(g)) ** 2) for g in
↪ [group1, group2, group3])

# Compute SST (Total sum of squares)
sst = ssb + ssw  # Alternatively, np.sum((data -
↪ grand_mean) ** 2)

# Perform \ac{anova} using SciPy
f_stat, p_value = stats.f_oneway(group1, group2, group3)

# Print results
print(f"SST (Total Sum of Squares): {sst:.4f}")
print(f"SSB (Between-Group Sum of Squares): {ssb:.4f}")
print(f"SSW (Within-Group Sum of Squares): {ssw:.4f}")
```

```
print(f"F-statistic: {f_stat:.4f}, pvalue:
↪   {p_value:.4f}")
```

The full executable code corresponding to this example is available online and can be accessed, reused, and commented on at: https://github.com/RiverPublishers/Computational-Approaches-in-Biology-and-Medicine/blob/main/Chapter3.ipynb

One of the main limitations of one-way ANOVA is that it is restricted to examining the effect of a *single independent factor* on a *single dependent variable.* While it is effective to detect if a statistically significant difference exists among the means of three or more groups, it does not identify *which of these groups* differ in mean. In other words, ANOVA can at most provide evidence that at least one group differs in mean; however, post hoc tests are required to determine which pairs of means exhibit significant differences.

3.2.3.2 Post-hoc tests

Post-hoc tests are used after a statistically significant one-way ANOVA to pinpoint which group means differ significantly. These tests control for the higher probability of making Type I errors arising from making multiple comparisons. Common post hoc methods include:

- *Tukey's honestly significant difference (HSD) test*: for all pairwise comparisons in mean between groups.
- *Dunnett's test*: for comparing each treatment group against one control group.
- *Analysis of means (ANOM)*: for comparing each group mean to the overall mean.

Each of these methods addresses different experimental questions and has specific assumptions about the data.

3.2.3.3 Tukey's Test

Tukey's honestly significant difference (HSD) test is a post hoc procedure used to perform pairwise comparisons between all group means following a statistically significant ANOVA result. It is designed to control the *Family-wise error rate (FWER)*, making sure that the overall risk of making one or more Type I errors across multiple comparisons remains within the specified significance level. HSD is especially suitable when the number of groups is moderate, and the assumption of equal variances holds. This test is appropriate under the following conditions:

- A one-way ANOVA has indicated a significant difference among group means.
- The data are normally distributed, and the groups have approximately equal variances.
- The sample sizes are equal or nearly equal (although the method can accommodate slight imbalances).
- The goal is to perform all the possible pairwise comparisons between group means while maintaining control over the overall Type I error rate.

3.2.3.4 Dunnett's test

Dunnett's test is a post hoc procedure specifically designed for situations where multiple treatment groups are compared against a single control group. Unlike methods that evaluate all possible pairwise comparisons (such as HSD), Dunnett's test focuses only on comparisons with the control, making it more statistically powerful in this context. By limiting the number of comparisons, it reduces the adjustment required for multiple testing, thereby increasing the sensitivity to detect meaningful differences between treatments and the control.

Example:

Imagine a study designed to evaluate how various drugs affect blood cell counts across three distinct groups of animals. The datasets below list the corresponding blood cell measurements, expressed in millions of cells per cubic millimetre.

```
import numpy as np

control = np.array([7.39, 8.46, 7.20, 8.36, 9.83, 8.26])
drug_a = np.array([9.78, 8.82, 7.68, 9.32])
drug_b = np.array([12.77, 9.76, 12.22, 9.16, 10.48])
```

The full executable code corresponding to this example is available online and can be accessed, reused, and commented on at: https://github.com/RiverPublishers/Computational-Approaches-in-Biology-and-Medicine/blob/main/Chapter3.ipynb

We consider the null hypothesis H_0 to state that the mean blood cell count in every treatment group is equal to the mean observed in the control group. The alternative hypothesis H_1 asserts that at least one of the drug-treated groups has a mean blood count that differs from the control. We will consider a 5% Family-wise error rate (FWER) to be acceptable (i.e., we choose $\alpha = 0.05$ as the threshold for significance). We apply Dunnett's test:

```
from scipy.stats import dunnett

res = dunnett(drug_a, drug_b, control=control)

print(f"pvalue: {res.pvalue}")
```

This yields: [0.62034889 0.00596362]

The full executable code corresponding to this example is available online and can be accessed, reused, and commented on at: https://github.com/RiverPublishers/Computational-Approaches-in-Biology-and-Medicine/blob/main/Chapter3.ipynb

The first p-value (0.62) is significantly higher than 0.05; thus, we cannot reject the null hypothesis. These results indicate that drug_a is not significantly different from the control. However, the second p-value (0.0059) suggests that drug_b causes a statistically significant change in blood count compared to the control group.

We can use this test when:

- We are comparing multiple treatment groups against a single control.
- ANOVA indicates an overall group effect.
- We want a powerful test with fewer comparisons.

3.3 Non-parametric Tests (Rank-based)

In biomedical data analysis, parametric tests such as the t-test may become unreliable when key assumptions, including normality and equal variances, are severely violated. In these situations, rank-based *non-parametric tests* provide a robust alternative [57, 58]. These methods operate on the ranks or relative order of the data values rather than their exact magnitudes, making them less sensitive to outliers and skewed distributions, and suitable for small or non-normally distributed samples.

In non-parametric settings, a one-sample test evaluates whether the median of a single group differs from a hypothesised value. In contrast, a two-sample test contrasts the distributions of two independent or paired groups. The choice depends on whether the data come from a single sample or involve a comparison between two related or independent samples.

3.3.1 Wilcoxon signed-rank test

The *Wilcoxon signed-rank test* is a non-parametric method used in place of the paired t-test [57]. It is used to evaluate whether the median difference between paired observations is significantly different from zero, for example, to assess changes in patients' biomarker levels before and after treatment. This test does not assume normality but does require that the differences are symmetrically distributed and that the observations are paired and independent. The procedure for conducting this test can be outlined as follows:

1. Compute the difference between each pair of related observations.
2. Exclude any pairs where the difference is exactly zero.
3. Rank the absolute values of the remaining (non-zero) differences from lowest to highest.
4. Reapply the original signs of the differences to their corresponding ranks.
5. Compute the sum of positive signed ranks and that of negative signed ranks.
6. The test statistic is the smaller of these two rank sums.

The following code snippet provides a simple example of a Wilcoxon signed-rank test in Python.

```
from scipy.stats import wilcoxon

# Pre- and post-treatment cholesterol levels
pre  = [200, 195, 180, 210, 190]
post = [185, 190, 178, 200, 188]

# Perform the Wilcoxon signed-rank test
stat, p-value = wilcoxon(pre, post)

# Print results
print(f"Wilcoxon statistic: {stat:.4f}, p-value:
↪  {p_value:.4f}")
```

The full executable code corresponding to this example is available online and can be accessed, reused, and commented on at: https://github.com/RiverPublishers/Computational-Approaches-in-Biology-and-Medicine/blob/main/Chapter3.ipynb

This test is particularly well-suited for evaluating changes in clinical measurements, such as blood pressure, cholesterol, or cytokine levels, when sample sizes are small or normality cannot be assumed.

3.3.2 Mann–Whitney U test

The *Mann–Whitney U test* (also known as the Wilcoxon rank-sum test) is a non-parametric alternative to the independent two-sample t-test [58].

It assesses whether one of two independent groups tends to display higher values than the other, making it especially effective when the data are skewed, ordinal, or non-normally distributed. This test assumes that observations are independent across groups, that the dependent variable is at least ordinal, and that the distributions of the two groups are similar (for interpretation based on medians). The procedure can be summarised as follows:

1. Combine and rank all values from both groups.
2. Calculate the sum of ranks for each group.
3. Compute the U statistic based on these rank sums.
4. Compare the U statistic to its sampling distribution under the null hypothesis.

This code snippet shows a simple example of a Mann–Whitney U test in Python.

```
from scipy.stats import mannwhitneyu

group1 = [7.1, 6.8, 7.5, 8.0]
group2 = [6.2, 5.9, 6.5, 6.8]

# Perform the Mann{Whitney U test
stat, p-value = mannwhitneyu(group1, group2,
 ↪  alternative='two-sided')

# Print results
print(f"Mann{Whitney U statistic: {stat}, p-value:
 ↪  {p-value}")
```

The full executable code corresponding to this example is available online and can be accessed, reused, and commented on at: https://github.com/RiverPublishers/Computational-Approaches-in-Biology-and-Medicine/blob/main/Chapter3.ipynb

The Mann–Whitney U test is frequently employed in biomedical research to compare the distributions of variables, such as gene expression, cytokine concentrations, or physiological measurements, between two independent groups (e.g., treatment vs. control) when parametric assumptions cannot be met.

3.3.3 Multi-group analysis

Multi-group analysis involves comparing more than two groups to assess whether they originate from the same distribution. In non-parametric settings, it is used when the assumptions of ANOVA are not met (e.g., non-normality or unequal variances), and the goal is to test for overall differences in central tendency or distribution across multiple independent or repeated-measures groups.

3.3.3.1 Kruskal–Wallis test

The *Kruskal–Wallis H test* is a non-parametric approach for assessing whether three or more independent groups differ in their underlying distributions. It serves as an alternative to one-way ANOVA, particularly in situations where the assumptions of normality and equal variances (homoscedasticity) are not met. This test extends the *Mann–Whitney U test* to multiple groups by ranking all observations across groups and examining whether the distribution of ranks significantly differs among them. A significant result suggests that at least one group has a distribution distinct from the others. Unlike ANOVA, the Kruskal–Wallis test does not assume equality of variances or normality of the data. It is generally used when the dependent variable is continuous or ordinal, the independent variable has three or more categories (e.g., different treatments or tissue types), the data violate normality or unequal variances assumptions, and the samples are independent and ideally have similarly shaped distributions.

This test can be summarised in the following steps:

1. Combine all group data and assign ranks to the pooled dataset.
2. Calculate the sum of ranks R_i for each group.
3. Compute the test statistic H:

$$H = \frac{12}{N(N+1)} \sum_{i=1}^{k} \frac{R_i^2}{n_i} - 3(N+1) \tag{3.9}$$

where:

- N is the total number of observations.
- k is the number of groups.
- n_i is the number of observations in group i.

4. The test statistic H approximately follows a chi-square distribution with $k - 1$ df.

```
from scipy.stats import kruskal

# Expression levels across three treatment groups
group1 = [5.2, 4.8, 5.1]
group2 = [6.0, 5.9, 6.2]
group3 = [7.1, 7.3, 7.0]

Perform the Kruskal{Wallis test
stat, p_value = kruskal(group1, group2, group3)

# Print results
print(f"Kruskal{Wallis H statistic: {stat}, p-value:
↪  {p_value}")
```

The full executable code corresponding to this example is available online and can be accessed, reused, and commented on at: https://github.com/RiverPublishers/Computational-Approaches-in-Biology-and-Medicine/blob/main/Chapter3.ipynb

Post-hoc analysis:

A significant Kruskal–Wallis result (e.g., $p < 0.05$) signals that at least one group is different from the others, but it does not reveal which pairs are different. In such cases, we can conduct pairwise Mann–Whitney U tests. Be sure to apply multiple-testing correction methods, such as the Bonferroni or Holm procedure, to control false positives (see the dedicated section on multiple testing corrections for details).

Kruskal–Wallis is well-suited for comparing gene expression levels across multiple tissue types, cytokine levels across disease stages (e.g., mild, moderate, severe), or functional or clinical scores across treatment groups. It is robust to non-normality, outliers, and differences in variances; thus, it can handle skewed data or small sample sizes. However, it may have lower statistical power than ANOVA when the data are truly normal, and it assumes that the group distributions are similarly shaped, allowing for interpretation based on medians.

3.3.3.2 Friedman test

The *Friedman test* is a non-parametric procedure for identifying differences among three or more related groups. It serves as the non-parametric analogue of repeated-measures ANOVA and is suited for situations in which the normality assumption does not hold. The test works by ranking the values within each subject (or block) across the different conditions and then analysing those ranks to determine whether the distributions differ across groups. This makes the Friedman test well-suited for within-subject designs or matched samples.

Example:

Consider a study in which the pulse rate (beats per minute) of seven students is measured at three time points:

- Before exercise: 72, 96, 88, 92, 74, 76, 82.
- Immediately after exercise: 120, 120, 132, 120, 101, 96, 112.
- Five minutes after exercise: 76, 95, 104, 96, 84, 72, 76.

The goal is to assess whether there is a significant change in pulse rate across these three conditions.

In Python, the Friedman test can be applied using the friedmanchisquare function from the scipy.stats module.

```
from scipy.stats import friedmanchisquare

before = [72, 95, 88, 93, 73, 75, 83]
immediately_after = [122, 120, 134, 120, 101, 97, 109]
five_min_after = [74, 95, 103, 97, 83, 71, 79]
res = friedmanchisquare(before, immediately_after,
↪  five_min_after)

print(f"Friedman statistic: {res.statistic:.4f}")
print(f"p-value: {res.pvalue:.6f}")
```

The full executable code corresponding to this example is available online and can be accessed, reused, and commented on at: https://github.com/RiverPublishers/Computational-Approaches-in-Biology-and-Medicine/blob/main/Chapter3.ipynb

Here are a few points for explanation and interpretation:

- The friedmanchisquare function tests the null hypothesis that the distributions of values across all conditions are identical.
- The function returns the test statistic and the value.
- If the p-value is less than the chosen significance level (commonly 0.05), we reject the null hypothesis, proving the existence of significant differences in pulse rates across the three time points in the samples.

3.4 Categorical Data Tests

Categorical data tests are used to analyse variables that represent categories or group memberships rather than numerical values [59]. These tests help determine whether distributions of categorical variables differ across groups or whether there are associations between them. In biomedical research, these tests are commonly used to evaluate outcomes such as disease presence, treatment response, and adverse events across patient groups. This section introduces the main methods for analysing categorical data: the chi-square test, Fisher's exact test, and OR analysis [60, 61].

3.4.1 Chi-square test

The *chi-square test* is a family of non-parametric tests used to assess whether observed categorical data significantly deviate from expected frequencies under a null model [60]. It is commonly used to test the *goodness-of-fit* of distributions or the *independence* of categorical variables in contingency tables.

3.4.1.1 Goodness-of-fit

The *chi-square goodness-of-fit* test evaluates whether the observed frequencies of a single categorical variable conform to a theoretical distribution. It is typically applied when we want to compare observed data with a theoretical or historical proportion.

Example:

Consider a scenario where we want to test if bags of candy contain equal numbers of each flavour (i.e., the expected frequencies are equal). The hypotheses would be:

- Null hypothesis (H_0): the proportions of candy flavours are equal (i.e., uniform distribution).
- Alternative hypothesis (H_1): the proportions of candy flavours are not equal.

The df for this test is calculated as the number of categories -1. For example, if there are five candy flavours: $df = 5 - 1 = 4$.

3.4.1.2 Test of independence

The *chi-square test of independence* is a statistical procedure employed to evaluate whether there exists a significant association between two categorical variables, or if they are independent of one another.

Example:

Suppose we want to determine if moviegoers' decisions to buy snacks depend on the type of movie being watched. The hypotheses would be:

- Null hypothesis (H_0): the proportion of people who buy snacks is independent of the movie type.
- Alternative hypothesis (H_1): the proportion of people who buy snacks varies with different movie types.

The df for this test are calculated as:

$$\begin{aligned} a &= \text{Number of categories for variable 1,} \\ b &= \text{Number of categories for variable 2,} \\ df &= (a - 1) \times (b - 1). \end{aligned} \tag{3.10}$$

For instance, if there are four movie genres and snack purchase is a yes/no variable: $df = (4 - 1) \times (2 - 1) = 3 \times 1 = 3$

The general procedure for conducting a chi-square test consists of the following steps:

1. State the null and alternative hypotheses.
2. Decide the significance level (α value), commonly set at 0.05.

3. Collect and check the data for errors.
4. Ensure the assumptions of the test are met, such as having a sufficient sample size and expected frequencies (e.g., at least 5 cells in most cell populations).
5. Calculate the test statistic:
$$\chi^2 = \sum \frac{(O_i - E_i)^2}{E_i}, \quad (3.11)$$
where O_i is the observed frequencies and E_i is the expected frequencies.
6. Compare the computed test statistic with the corresponding critical value from the chi-square distribution, using the appropriate df, to decide whether the null hypothesis should be rejected.

In statistical analysis, the *chi-square distribution* refers to a family of probability distributions, each defined by a specific number of df. As the df increase, the shape of the distribution becomes more symmetric and gradually approaches that of the *standard normal distribution* (also known as the *z-distribution*). The figure below illustrates how the shape of the chi-square distribution evolves with increasing df, using three representative curves generated in Python.

```
import numpy as np
import matplotlib.pyplot as plt
import seaborn as sns
from scipy.stats import chi2

np.random.seed(42)

# Set publication-style aesthetics
sns.set_theme(style="whitegrid", context="talk")

# Define the range for the x-axis
x = np.linspace(0, 20, 500)

# Define degrees of freedom
dfs = [3, 4, 8]
colours = sns.color_palette("dark", n_colors=len(dfs))

# Create the figure
plt.figure(figsize=(10, 6))

# Plot chi-square distributions
for df, colour in zip(dfs, colours):
plt.plot(x, chi2.pdf(x, df), label=f'df = {df}',
 ↪   color=colour, linewidth=2.5)
```

```
# Add title, labels, grid, and legend
plt.xlabel('x', fontsize=16)
plt.ylabel('Probability Density', fontsize=16)
plt.title('Chi-square Distributions', fontsize=20,
 ↪  fontweight='bold')
plt.legend(frameon=True, fontsize=14)
plt.grid(True, linestyle='--', alpha=0.6)
sns.despine()

# Show the plot
plt.tight_layout()
plt.show()
```

The full executable code corresponding to this example is available online and can be accessed, reused, and commented on at: https://github.com/RiverPublishers/Computational-Approaches-in-Biology-and-Medicine/blob/main/Chapter3.ipynb

Figure 3.2: Three chi-square distributions generated by varying the df.

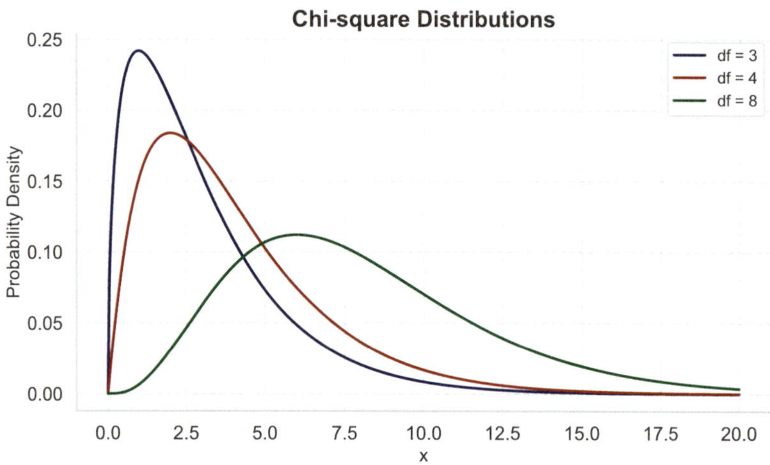

As shown in the plot in Figure 3.2, chi-square distributions become more symmetric and bell-shaped as the df increase.

3.4.2 Fisher's exact test

The *Fisher's exact test* is a statistical method used to assess whether two categorical variables are statistically associated, particularly in 2×2 contingency tables with small sample sizes [61]. Unlike the chi-square test, it does not rely on large-sample approximations; instead, it computes an exact p-value under the null hypothesis of independence.

To illustrate this approach, we examine a clinical study designed to assess the efficacy of acetazolamide 250 mg in averting acute mountain sickness (AMS). The research involved two participant groups: one group received acetazolamide, while the other received a placebo. The study tracked and documented the incidence of Acute mountain sickness (AMS) across both groups as in Table 3.1. The goal is to assess whether acetazolamide reduces the risk of AMS compared to the placebo.

Table 3.1: Contingency table for the AMS study.

	AMS cases	No AMS cases	Total
Acetazolamide	7	15	22
Placebo	17	5	22
Total	24	20	44

In Python, Fisher's exact test can be applied using the fisher_exact function from the scipy.stats module. Below is the corresponding code:

```
from scipy.stats import fisher_exact

# Contingency table: [ [AMS, No AMS], ... ]
table = [[7, 15], [17, 5]]

# One-sided Fisher's exact test (testing for reduction
↪ in AMS with treatment)
oddsratio, p_value = fisher_exact(table,
↪ alternative='less')

print(f"Odds ratio: {oddsratio:.4f}")
print(f"P-value: {p_value:.4f}")
```

The full executable code corresponding to this example is available online and can be accessed, reused, and commented on at: https://github.com/RiverPublishers/Computational-Approaches-in-Biology-and-Medicine/blob/main/Chapter3.ipynb

Here are a few points for explanation and interpretation:

- Table 3.1 displays the contingency table of observed frequencies;
- The alternative='less' parameter indicates a one-sided test, where the alternative hypothesis posits that the odds of AMS are lower in the acetazolamide group compared to the placebo group;
- The function calculates and returns the OR and the p-value.

If the p-value falls below the selected significance threshold (commonly 0.05), the null hypothesis is rejected, indicating that acetazolamide leads to a meaningful reduction in the risk of acute mountain sickness relative to the placebo.

3.5 Variance Homogeneity Tests

Assessing the equality of variances across groups, also known as *homogeneity of variance* or *homoscedasticity*, is a key assumption in many parametric tests, including ANOVA and the t-test. Violations of this assumption can lead to *misleading p-values* and *incorrect conclusions. Variance homogeneity tests* are used to determine whether the *spread of values* differs significantly between groups [62]. This section introduces commonly used tests for this purpose, including Levene's test, Bartlett's test, and the Fligner–Killeen test, each with different sensitivities to non-normality and outliers.

3.5.1 Levene's test

Levene's test is a statistical method used to assess whether two or more groups have the same variance (i.e., homoscedasticity) [63]. It is commonly applied prior to parametric tests, such as ANOVA or t-tests, which assume equal variances across groups. Unlike other methods, it is robust to non-normality, making it a viable choice in a variety of real-world biomedical studies.

The *null hypothesis* H_0 in Levene's test is that all group variances are equal. Suppose the resulting p-value of Levene's test is less than a chosen significance level (typically 0.05). In that case, it suggests that at least one group has a variance that differs significantly from the others.

Example:

Consider a study aimed at assessing how different daily doses of vitamin C influence tooth growth in guinea pigs. In this controlled setting, 60 animals were randomly allocated to one of three treatment conditions: a *low dose* of 0.5 mg/day, a *medium dose* of 1.0 mg/day, and a *high dose* of 2.0 mg/day. Each group received its respective dosage daily for 42 days, after which tooth growth was measured for each subject. Thus, the subjects are divided into three groups, each receiving a different daily dose:

- Small dose (0.5 mg): 4.3, 11.5, 7.6, 6.4, 6.3, 10.0, 11.9, 11.6, 5.0, 7.2, 15.2, 21.6, 17.9, 9.0, 13.9, 9.8, 7.8, 9.6, 16.3, 9.2
- Medium dose (1.0 mg): 17.2, 16.5, 15.4, 16.9, 22.4, 17.5, 13.3, 14.8, 18.7, 15.5, 19.6, 24.1, 23.7, 26.0, 20.4, 24.8, 25.9, 20.5, 14.1, 27.4
- Large dose (2.0 mg): 23.8, 18.4, 34.1, 25.4, 25.8, 32.4, 26.5, 21.8, 23.4, 28.9, 25.6, 26.3, 22.0, 24.7, 25.2, 31.4, 26.1, 27.2, 29.6, 23.3.

The objective is to determine whether the variances in tooth growth differ significantly between the dose groups. In Python, Levene's test can be performed using the levene function from the scipy.stats module.

```
import numpy as np
from scipy import stats

small_dose = np.array([4.3, 11.5, 7.6, 6.4, 6.3, 10.0,
↪  11.9, 11.6, 5.0, 7.2, 15.2, 21.6, 17.9, 9.0, 13.9,
↪  9.8, 7.8, 9.6, 16.3, 9.2])
medium_dose = np.array([17.2, 16.5, 15.4, 16.9, 22.4,
↪  17.5, 13.3, 14.8, 18.7, 15.5, 19.6, 24.1, 23.7,
↪  26.0, 20.4, 24.8, 25.9, 20.5, 14.1, 27.4])
large_dose = np.array([23.8, 18.4, 34.1, 25.4, 25.8,
↪  32.4, 26.5, 21.8, 23.4, 28.9, 25.6, 26.3, 22.0,
↪  24.7, 25.2, 31.4, 26.1, 27.2, 29.6, 23.3])

res = stats.levene(small_dose, medium_dose, large_dose)

print(f"Levene's test statistic: {res.statistic:.4f}")
print(f"P-value: {res.pvalue:.4f}")
```

The full executable code corresponding to this example is available online and can be accessed, reused, and commented on at: https://github.com/RiverPublishers/Computational-Approaches-in-Biology-and-Medicine/blob/main/Chapter3.ipynb

Here are a few points for explanation and interpretation:

- Test statistic: this quantifies the variation in spread (deviations) among groups.
- p-value: the probability of observing this level of variation if the group variances are truly equal.

If the p-value is below the selected significance level (typically 0.05), the null hypothesis is rejected, indicating that at least one group exhibits a variance that differs significantly from the others.

3.5.2 Bartlett's test

Bartlett's test is a statistical procedure used to determine whether the variances across two or more groups are equal [64]. Like Levene's test, it is commonly applied to evaluate the assumption of *equality of variance*, which underlies many parametric methods. However, Bartlett's test is highly sensitive to deviations from normality and is therefore most appropriate when the data are approximately normally distributed.

Example:

For consistency and ease of comparison across methods, we will use the same vitamin C dosage example on guinea pig tooth growth. In Python, Bartlett's test can be performed using the bartlett function from the scipy.stats module.

```
import numpy as np
from scipy import stats

small_dose = np.array([4.3, 11.5, 7.6, 6.4, 6.3, 10.0,
 ↪  11.9, 11.6, 5.0, 7.2, 15.2, 21.6, 17.9, 9.0, 13.9,
 ↪  9.8, 7.8, 9.6, 16.3, 9.2])
medium_dose = np.array([17.2, 16.5, 15.4, 16.9, 22.4,
 ↪  17.5, 13.3, 14.8, 18.7, 15.5, 19.6, 24.1, 23.7,
 ↪  26.0, 20.4, 24.8, 25.9, 20.5, 14.1, 27.4])
large_dose = np.array([23.8, 18.4, 34.1, 25.4, 25.8,
 ↪  32.4, 26.5, 21.8, 23.4, 28.9, 25.6, 26.3, 22.0,
 ↪  24.7, 25.2, 31.4, 26.1, 27.2, 29.6, 23.3])
```

```
res = stats.bartlett(small_dose, medium_dose,
 ↪  large_dose)
print(f"Bartlett's test statistic: {res.statistic:.4f}")
print(f"P-value: {res.pvalue:.4f}")
```

The full executable code corresponding to this example is available online and can be accessed, reused, and commented on at: https://github.com/RiverPublishers/Computational-Approaches-in-Biology-and-Medicine/blob/main/Chapter3.ipynb

Under the null hypothesis, the test statistic is approximately chi-square distributed with $k - 1$ df, where k denotes the number of groups. A large test statistic paired with a small p-value suggests that the variances differ significantly across groups. Figure 3.3 illustrates this distribution for $k = 3$.

```
import numpy as np
import matplotlib.pyplot as plt
import seaborn as sns
from scipy.stats import chi2

np.random.seed(42)

# Set publication-style aesthetics
sns.set_theme(style="whitegrid", context="talk")

# Number of samples
k = 3
dist = stats.chi2(df=k-1)
val  = np.linspace(0, 5, 100)
pdf  = dist.pdf(val)

colours = sns.color_palette("dark")

# Create the figure
plt.figure(figsize=(10, 6))

plt.plot(val, pdf, color=colours[0])
plt.xlim(0, 5)
plt.ylim(0, 1)

# Add title, labels, and grid
plt.xlabel('Statistic', fontsize=16)
```

```
plt.ylabel('Probability density function', fontsize=16)
plt.title('Bartlett Test Null Distribution',
↪  fontsize=20, fontweight='bold')
plt.grid(True, linestyle='--', alpha=0.6)
sns.despine()

# Show the plot
plt.tight_layout()
plt.show()
```

The full executable code corresponding to this example is available online and can be accessed, reused, and commented on at: https://github.com/RiverPublishers/Computational-Approaches-in-Biology-and-Medicine/blob/main/Chapter3.ipynb

Figure 3.3: Chi-Square distribution with two df.

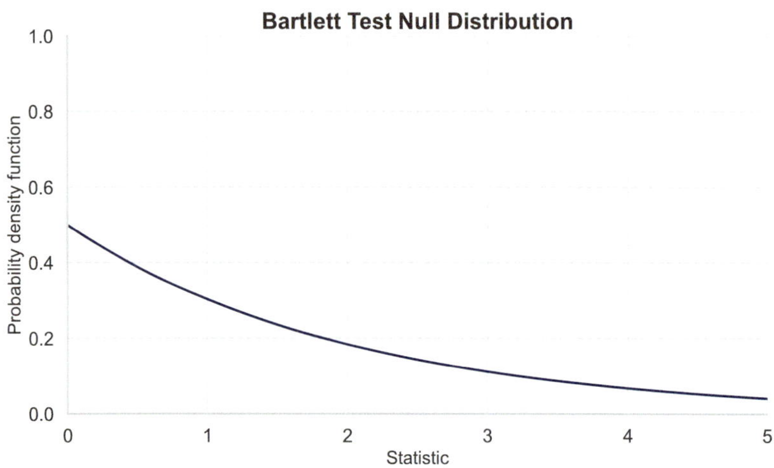

A low p-value (typically <0.05) would indicate that the group variances differ significantly. In our example, the p-value of 0.41 is not significant, suggesting no strong evidence to reject the null hypothesis of equal variances.

3.5.3 Fligner–Killeen test

The *Fligner–Killeen test* is a non-parametric approach for evaluating whether the variances of two or more groups are equal [65]. It is particularly useful when the assumption of normality cannot be guaranteed, as it is more robust than both Bartlett's and Levene's tests in the presence of outliers or skewed distributions.

Example:

Let's reconsider the vitamin C dosage example related to guinea pig tooth growth. In Python, the Fligner–Killeen test can be performed using the fligner function from the scipy.stats module.

```
import numpy as np

small_dose = np.array([4.3, 11.5, 7.6, 6.4, 6.3, 10.0,
↪  11.9, 11.6, 5.0, 7.2, 15.2, 21.6, 17.9, 9.0, 13.9,
↪  9.8, 7.8, 9.6, 16.3, 9.2])
medium_dose = np.array([17.2, 16.5, 15.4, 16.9, 22.4,
↪  17.5, 13.3, 14.8, 18.7, 15.5, 19.6, 24.1, 23.7,
↪  26.0, 20.4, 24.8, 25.9, 20.5, 14.1, 27.4])
large_dose = np.array([23.8, 18.4, 34.1, 25.4, 25.8,
↪  32.4, 26.5, 21.8, 23.4, 28.9, 25.6, 26.3, 22.0,
↪  24.7, 25.2, 31.4, 26.1, 27.2, 29.6, 23.3])

from scipy import stats

res = stats.fligner(small_dose, medium_dose, large_dose)
print(f"Fligner-Killeen's test statistic:
↪  {res.statistic:.4f}")
print(f"P-value: {res.pvalue:.4f}")
```

The full executable code corresponding to this example is available online and can be accessed, reused, and commented on at: https://github.com/RiverPublishers/Computational-Approaches-in-Biology-and-Medicine/blob/main/Chapter3.ipynb

As with the previous tests, a low p-value (typically <0.05) indicates that at least one group has a significantly different variance. A high p-value (like in this example) means there is no strong evidence to reject the null hypothesis of equality of variances.

Levene's test is generally preferred over Bartlett's test when the assumption of normality is questionable, as it is more robust to departures from normal distributions. Bartlett's test, on the other hand, is most appropriate when the data are known to be normally distributed. Due to its strong robustness to both non-normality and outliers, the Fligner–Killeen test is particularly well-suited for exploratory biomedical analyses or when the distributional properties of the data are unknown or potentially problematic.

3.6 Multiple Testing Corrections

When performing a *large number of statistical tests*, such as in pairwise group comparisons, omics analyses, or exploratory studies, the probability of obtaining *false positives* increases rapidly. This phenomenon, known as the *multiple testing problem*, inflates the overall *Type I error rate* if not properly controlled. To address this issue, multiple testing correction methods adjust significance thresholds to control either the probability of making at least one false positive (the *FWER*) or the expected proportion of false positives among the rejected hypotheses (the *False discovery rate (FDR)*). This section introduces two widely used correction approaches: the *Bonferroni correction* [66], which is simple but conservative, and the *Benjamini–Hochberg procedure (BH)* [67], which controls the FDR and is well suited for high-dimensional data such as those encountered in genomics and transcriptomics.

Failure to apply these corrections can result in irreproducible findings and overstated scientific claims. Moreover, *publication bias*, the tendency to publish positive findings more readily than null results, can further distort the literature. To mitigate these effects, researchers are encouraged to pre-register hypotheses, report all tested comparisons transparently, and apply appropriate correction strategies when interpreting results.

3.6.1 Bonferroni correction

The *Bonferroni correction* is a commonly applied technique for controlling the FWER. It modifies the significance level by dividing the selected α by the total number of tests m. In doing so, it keeps the chance of committing at least one Type I error across all comparisons at or below the desired level.

$$\alpha_{\text{adjusted}} = \frac{\alpha}{m}.$$

For example, if 10 independent tests are performed with a standard significance level of $\alpha = 0.05$, the Bonferroni-adjusted threshold becomes $\alpha_{\text{adjusted}} = 0.005$. Any individual test must have a p-value less than this threshold to be considered statistically significant.

The Bonferroni correction is easy to implement and interpret, but it can be overly conservative, especially when a large number of tests are performed or when tests are correlated. In such cases, the likelihood of false negatives (Type II errors) increases, potentially masking true effects.

We can use this correction when:

- The number of tests is small.
- Controlling even a single false positive is critical.
- Tests are independent or nearly independent.

3.6.2 Benjamini–Hochberg Procedure

The *Benjamini–Hochberg procedure (BH)* is a method used to control the FDR, the expected proportion of false positives among the set of rejected hypotheses. Unlike the Bonferroni correction, which controls the chance of any false positives, the BH procedure allows for a controlled proportion of false discoveries, making it more powerful in situations involving many simultaneous tests. The BH procedure works as follows:

1. Order all m p-values from smallest to largest: $p_{(1)}, p_{(2)}, \ldots, p_{(m)}$.
2. Find the largest k such that:
$$p_{(k)} \leq \frac{k}{m} \cdot \alpha.$$
3. Reject all null hypotheses corresponding to $p_{(1)}, p_{(2)}, \ldots, p_{(k)}$.

The BH procedure is particularly well-suited for fields such as genomics, where thousands of statistical tests are performed in a single experiment. It strikes a balance between discovery and reliability, reducing the risk of both false positives and false negatives.

We can use this procedure when:

- A large number of hypotheses are tested.
- Some false positives are tolerable, but reproducibility is still important.
- Tests may be dependent or weakly correlated.

3.7 Assumption Checking and Distribution Tests

Before applying many statistical methods, especially parametric tests, it is essential to evaluate whether key assumptions hold. Such assumptions often include the normality of the data distribution, symmetry, and homogeneity of variance [68, 69]. Violating them can lead to biased estimates, incorrect p-values, and reduced statistical power. This section introduces common tests for evaluating the distributional properties of data, including the Shapiro–Wilk test for normality, as well as tests for skewness and kurtosis to assess asymmetry and tail behaviour. In practice, these formal tests are often complemented by visual inspection techniques such as histograms, boxplots, or Q–Q plots (Figure 3.4), which help identify potential deviations from expected distributional shapes.

```
import numpy as np
import matplotlib.pyplot as plt
import scipy.stats as stats
import seaborn as sns

np.random.seed(42)

# Set publication-style aesthetics
sns.set_theme(style="whitegrid", context="talk")

# Example: generate sample data
data = np.random.normal(loc=0, scale=1, size=100)   #
↪  Normally distributed

# Create the figure
plt.figure(figsize=(10, 6))

# Generate Q{Q plot
stats.probplot(data, dist="norm", plot=plt)

# Add title, labels, and grid
plt.xlabel('Theoretical Quantiles', fontsize=16)
plt.ylabel('Sample Quantiles', fontsize=16)
plt.title('Q{Q Plot for Normality Check', fontsize=20,
↪  fontweight='bold')
plt.grid(True, linestyle='--', alpha=0.6)
sns.despine()

# Show the plot
plt.tight_layout()
plt.show()
```

The full executable code corresponding to this example is available online and can be accessed, reused, and commented on at: https://github.com/RiverPublishers/Computational-Approaches-in-Biology-and-Medicine/blob/main/Chapter3.ipynb

Figure 3.4: Q-Q plot contrasting the sample quantiles with those of a theoretical normal distribution. When the plotted points lie near the diagonal reference line, the data can be regarded as roughly consistent with normality. Systematic deviations from the line may indicate skewness, kurtosis, or other departures from normality.

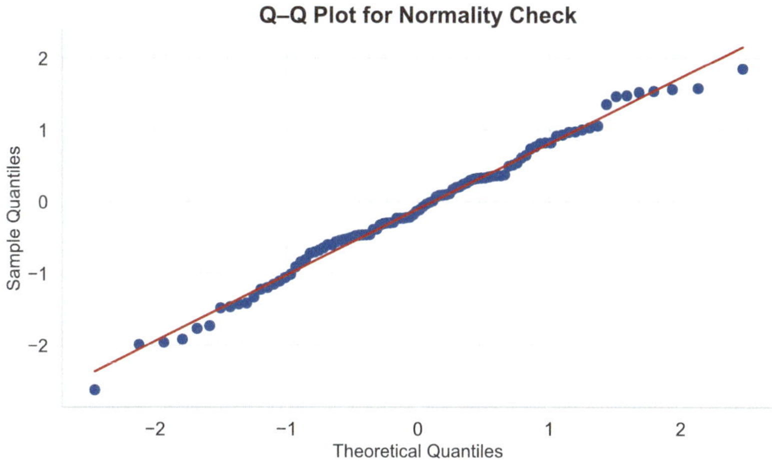

3.7.1 Shapiro–Wilk test

The *Shapiro–Wilk test* is a commonly used statistical method for assessing whether a sample originates from a normally distributed population [68]. It tests the null hypothesis that the data follow a normal distribution and is frequently employed to verify normality assumptions required by many parametric analyses.

Example:

Consider a study measuring the weights (in pounds) of adult human males. The recorded weights are:

$$148, 154, 158, 160, 161, 162, 166, 170, 182, 195, 236.$$

The objective is to determine whether these weights are normally distributed. To perform the Shapiro–Wilk test in Python, we can use the shapiro function from the scipy.stats module.

```
import numpy as np
from scipy import stats

x = np.array([148, 154, 158, 160, 161, 162, 166, 170,
↪  182, 195, 236])

res = stats.shapiro(x)
print(f"Test statistic: {res.statistic:.4f}")
print(f"P-value: {res.pvalue:.4f}")
```

The full executable code corresponding to this example is available online and can be accessed, reused, and commented on at: https://github.com/RiverPublishers/Computational-Approaches-in-Biology-and-Medicine/blob/main/Chapter3.ipynb

Here are a few points for explanation and interpretation:

- **Test statistic:** A value near 1 suggests that the sample closely follows a normal distribution, whereas values that deviate significantly from 1 indicate potential departures from normality.
- **p-value:** If the p-value is below the selected significance level (typically 0.05), the null hypothesis is rejected, indicating that the data is unlikely to follow a normal distribution.

In the example considered, the p-value is less than 0.05. Therefore, we reject the null hypothesis and infer that the sample is unlikely to be from a normal distribution. The Shapiro–Wilk test is particularly effective for small to moderate sample sizes ($n < 50$). However, it may become overly sensitive in large samples, detecting trivial deviations from normality as statistically significant.

3.7.2 Kurtosis test

The *kurtosis test* assesses whether the tail behaviour (tailedness) of a dataset deviates significantly from that of a normal distribution [70]. It tests the null hypothesis that the sample kurtosis matches the kurtosis of a normal distribution. This test is particularly useful in assessing the presence of outliers or the heaviness of the tails in the data distribution.

Example:

For consistency and ease of comparison across methods, we use the same example dataset as in the previous section.

In Python, the kurtosis test can be performed using the kurtosistest function from the scipy.stats module.

```
import numpy as np
from scipy import stats

x = np.array([146, 152, 159, 161, 163, 164, 167, 171,
 ↪ 184, 198, 240])

res = stats.kurtosistest(x)
print(f"Kurtosis test statistic: {res.statistic:.4f}")
print(f"P-value: {res.pvalue:.6f}")
```

The full executable code corresponding to this example is available online and can be accessed, reused, and commented on at: https://github.com/RiverPublishers/Computational-Approaches-in-Biology-and-Medicine/blob/main/Chapter3.ipynb

Here are a few points for explanation:

- Test statistic: the computed z-score indicates how much the sample kurtosis deviates from the kurtosis of a normal distribution.
- p-value: If the p-value is below the selected significance level (typically 0.05), the null hypothesis is rejected, suggesting that the data have significantly different tail behaviour, either heavier or lighter, than a normal distribution.

The kurtosis test is most reliable with larger sample sizes. For small datasets (e.g., fewer than 20 observations), results should be interpreted with caution due to limited power.

3.7.3 Skewness test

The *skewness test* evaluates whether the asymmetry of a dataset differs significantly from that of a normal distribution, which has a skewness of zero [70]. It tests the null hypothesis that the population distribution is symmetric.

Example:

For consistency and ease of comparison across methods, we use the same dataset as in the previous tests. To perform the skewness test in Python, we can use the skewtest function from the scipy.stats module.

```
import numpy as np
from scipy import stats

x = np.array([146, 152, 159, 161, 163, 164, 167, 171,
↪  184, 198, 240])

res = stats.skewtest(x)
print(f"Skewness test statistic: {res.statistic:.4f}")
print(f"P-value: {res.pvalue:.4f}")
```

The full executable code corresponding to this example is available online and can be accessed, reused, and commented on at: https://github.com/RiverPublishers/Computational-Approaches-in-Biology-and-Medicine/blob/main/Chapter3.ipynb

Here are a few points for explanation and interpretation:

- Test statistic: the computed z-score indicates how much the sample's skewness deviates from the expected skewness of a normal distribution.
- p-value: If the p-value is less than the chosen significance level (commonly 0.05), we reject the null hypothesis, indicating that the data are significantly skewed and deviate from symmetry.

The test requires a minimum of eight observations, and for small samples, the p-value may be inaccurate, yielding unreliable results.

3.8 Correlation Analysis

Correlation analysis quantifies both the strength and the direction of the relationship between two continuous variables. [71]. It is a fundamental tool in exploratory data analysis and predictive modelling. However, *correlation does not imply causation*: two variables may be correlated due to a third confounding variable, reverse causality, or purely by chance. Interpreting correlations carefully is especially crucial in biomedical research, where both biological plausibility and study design must be considered.

3.8.1 Pearson Correlation

The *Pearson correlation coefficient*, denoted by r, is a parametric statistic that captures the strength and direction of a linear association between two continuous variables [72]. Statistical testing of the coefficient requires assuming that the variables are normally distributed, have a linear relationship, and are homoscedastic.

The coefficient r is calculated as:

$$r = \frac{\sum(x_i - \bar{x})(y_i - \bar{y})}{\sqrt{\sum(x_i - \bar{x})^2 \sum(y_i - \bar{y})^2}}.$$

Values of r range from -1 to 1:

- $r = 1$: perfect positive linear correlation
- $r = -1$: perfect negative linear correlation
- $r = 0$: no linear correlation.

Example:

Consider a study that examines how *free proline* (an amino acid) relates to *total collagen* (a major structural protein in connective tissue) in human livers affected by disease. The data consist of measurements of total collagen (expressed in mg/g of dry liver weight) and free proline (expressed in mole/g of dry liver weight) for each sample:

- Total collagen: 7.1, 7.1, 7.2, 8.3, 9.4, 10.5, 11.4;
- Free proline: 2.8, 2.9, 2.8, 2.6, 3.5, 4.6, 5.0.

In Python, we compute Pearson's correlation using the pearsonr function.

```
import numpy as np
from scipy.stats import pearsonr

# Total collagen (mg/g dry weight of liver)
x = np.array([7.0, 7.3, 7.3, 8.1, 9.4, 10.9, 11.1])

# Free proline (μ mole/g dry weight of liver)
y = np.array([2.7, 3.1, 2.8, 2.5, 3.5, 4.9, 4.7])

# Compute the Pearson correlation
```

```
res = pearsonr(x, y)
print(f"Pearson correlation coefficient:
↪  {res.statistic:.4f}")
print(f"P-value: {res.pvalue:.4f}")
```

The full executable code corresponding to this example is available online and can be accessed, reused, and commented on at: https://github.com/RiverPublishers/Computational-Approaches-in-Biology-and-Medicine/blob/main/Chapter3.ipynb

We can use the Pearson correlation when:

- We expect a linear relationship between two continuous variables.
- Data are approximately normally distributed.
- Outliers are minimal or properly handled.

3.8.2 Spearman correlation

The *Spearman rank-order correlation coefficient*, typically written as ρ (rho), is a non-parametric measure used to assess the strength and direction of a *monotonic* relationship between two variables [73]. Instead of working with the original data values, it is computed from their ranks, which allows it to characterise monotonic associations that need not follow a linear pattern.

Example:

Let's consider the previous example on the total collagen measurements. The objective is to determine the strength and direction of the monotonic relationship between free proline and total collagen levels. To compute Spearman's rank correlation coefficient in Python, we use the spearmanr function from the scipy.stats module

```
import numpy as np
from scipy import stats

# Total collagen (mg/g dry weight of liver)
x = np.array([7.0, 7.3, 7.3, 8.1, 9.4, 10.9, 11.1])

# Free proline (μ mole/g dry weight of liver)
y = np.array([2.7, 3.1, 2.8, 2.5, 3.5, 4.9, 4.7])
```

```python
# Compute the Spearman correlation
res = stats.spearmanr(x, y)
print(f"Spearman correlation coefficient:
↪  {res.statistic:.4f}")
print(f"P-value: {res.pvalue:.4f}")
```

The full executable code corresponding to this example is available online and can be accessed, reused, and commented on at: https://github.com/RiverPublishers/Computational-Approaches-in-Biology-and-Medicine/blob/main/Chapter3.ipynb

Here are a few points for explanation and interpretation:

- *Spearman's correlation coefficient* (ρ) takes values between -1 and $+1$. A value close to $+1$ signifies a strong *positive* monotonic association, where increases in one variable are typically accompanied by increases in the other. A value near -1 signals a strong *negative* monotonic association, meaning that larger values of one variable tend to correspond to smaller values of the other. Values around 0 indicate that the variables show little to no monotonic relationship.
- **p-value:** This quantifies the evidence against the null hypothesis that the two variables are independent. A small p-value (typically less than 0.05) indicates that the observed correlation is unlikely to have occurred by chance and is therefore considered statistically significant.

We can use this when:

- You expect a monotonic relationship, but not necessarily linear.
- Your data are ordinal, skewed, or contain outliers.
- The assumption of normality is not satisfied.

Additional notes:

Another rank-based correlation measure is the *Kendall* τ coefficient, which is based on the number of concordant and discordant pairs [74]. It is often more conservative than Spearman and may be preferred in datasets with many tied ranks or small sample sizes.

In biomedical studies, it is common to report both Pearson and Spearman correlation coefficients to account for the different characteristics of the data. For instance, while Pearson's correlation may indicate a moderate linear association between C-reactive protein (CRP) levels and disease severity, Spearman's or Kendall's correlation may reveal a stronger monotonic relationship, particularly when distributions are skewed. It is essential to remember that correlation only reflects association, not causality—confounding variables, reverse causation, or bias may explain observed trends.

CHAPTER

4

Machine Learning in Biomedical Research

ML is an interdisciplinary field that lies at the intersection of computer science, statistics, and applied mathematics [75, 76]. It focuses on developing algorithms that enable computers to learn patterns and make informed decisions based on data. ML has evolved alongside advances in computational power, data availability, and algorithmic innovations. Historically, the field began with basic pattern recognition and statistical analysis, but it has since undergone significant transformations through breakthroughs in areas such as neural networks and deep learning. Nowadays, ML is ubiquitous across diverse fields, including healthcare, finance, robotics, and natural language processing, driving innovation and efficiency in complex, data-intensive environments. The growth of big data and the advent of cloud computing have further catalysed the evolution of ML, enabling the processing of massive datasets and the training of large models with unprecedented complexity.

This chapter begins by introducing basic ML concepts and then delves deeper into the main families of models. Similar to the previous chapter, it includes code snippets in Python, primarily using the sklearn library, to provide hands-on examples.

4.1 Different Machine Learning Approaches

ML can be broadly categorised into three main paradigms, each with distinct methodologies and applications.

10.1201/9788743812487-6

- **Supervised learning**: Models are trained on a *labelled dataset*, where each input is paired with a corresponding output. The objective is to learn a *mapping from inputs to outputs*, enabling the model to predict the correct label for new, unseen data. Thus, supervised ML models are generally trained by minimising a *loss function* that quantifies the model fit. Common applications include classification tasks, such as image recognition, and regression tasks, such as forecasting economic indicators.
- **Unsupervised learning**: Unlike supervised learning, unsupervised learning deals with *unlabeled data*. The goal is to identify *underlying structures* or *patterns* within the data, such as grouping similar items (clustering) or reducing the dimensionality of the data (dimensionality reduction). This approach is particularly useful in exploratory data analysis and in discovering *hidden relationships* in complex datasets.
- **Reinforcement learning (RL)**: In this learning framework, an *agent* learns to *make decisions* by interacting with an *environment*. The agent receives *feedback* in the form of *rewards* or *penalties* based on its *actions* and iteratively adjusts its behaviour to maximise cumulative rewards. This learning strategy is particularly relevant in dynamic and sequential decision-making tasks, such as those found in robotics and autonomous navigation.

Most supervised ML algorithms work by defining a *loss function*, which measures how far the model's predictions deviate from the observed outcomes. The model is then trained to minimise such loss. For example, linear regression minimises the mean squared error (MSE), logistic regression (LR) maximises the likelihood (which can be viewed as minimising the log-loss), and classification trees minimise impurity measures like the Gini index or entropy. Thinking in terms of loss functions allows unifying diverse models under a common optimisation framework. While Reinforcement learning (RL) is gaining relevance in the modern ML landscape (e.g., in training large language models), it falls outside the scope of this book. Therefore, in the next sections, we will primarily discuss the supervised and unsupervised paradigms.

4.1.1 Fundamental assumptions

Before exploring various models for each paradigm, we outline the primary theoretical assumptions that underpin all ML algorithms. Firstly, there is the assumption of *data representativeness*: the *training data* must sufficiently capture the *underlying distribution* of the *real-world phenomena* to which the model is expected to generalise. Secondly, many ML techniques operate under the assumption of *independent and identically distributed data points*, which simplifies model design and interpretation; however, this assumption may not always hold in practice with real-world data. Finally, the concept of *bias and variance trade-off* assumes that every learning algorithm must strike a *balance* between *complexity* and *generalisability* to avoid *overfitting* or *underfitting*. Recognising these assumptions is critical for both the effective design of ML models and the proper interpretation of their results.

4.2 Supervised Learning

The following section will explore the various categories of models that can be used in supervised learning settings, beginning with the simple *linear regression model* and progressing to more complex *nonlinear models*. For each model, mathematical formulations, key assumptions, and detailed working principles are discussed.

4.2.1 Training, validation, and test sets

Good generalisation requires proper data partitioning. Biomedical datasets are often small or high-dimensional, which increases the risk of overfitting and data leakage if they are not handled properly. Model training requires dividing data into three distinct sets:

- **Training set**: Used to fit (i.e., learn) the model parameters.
- **Validation set**: Used for hyperparameter tuning, evaluating different models, and preventing overfitting.
- **Test set**: Held out and used only once to evaluate the final model performance.

Common error: Using the test set to make modelling decisions (e.g., choosing features, adjusting parameters) leaks information and invalidates performance estimates. Thus, failing to respect this separation leads to *data leakage*, often causing *overly optimistic results*.

Tip: If your dataset is too small to have a separate validation set, use CV (see Section 4.5.3) instead of a *fixed split*.

4.2.2 Linear regression

Linear regression is one of the simplest and most *interpretable* supervised learning models, used for predicting *continuous outcomes*. The fundamental idea is to model the relationship between a dependent variable y and one or more independent variables $\mathrm{x} = (x_1, x_2, \ldots, x_m)$ using a linear equation with the form:

$$y = \theta_0 + \theta_1 x_1 + \theta_2 x_2 + \cdots + \theta_m x_m + \epsilon, \tag{4.1}$$

where θ_0 is the *intercept*, $\theta_1, \ldots, \theta_m$ are the *coefficients*, and ϵ is an *error term*. The goal of training this model is to estimate the set of parameters $\theta_0, \theta_1, \ldots, \theta_m$ which guarantee the best fit to the original dataset. The most common approach is the *Ordinary least squares (OLS)* method, in which the *residual sum of squares* between the *observed targets* in the training dataset and the *targets* predicted by the linear approximation is minimised across all data points:

$$\min_{\beta_0, \beta_1, \ldots, \beta_m} \sum_{i=1}^{m} \left(y_i - \beta_0 - \sum_{j=1}^{p} \beta_j x_{ij} \right)^2 . \tag{4.2}$$

In a more compact vector notation, this is normally written as:

$$\min_{\beta} \|X\theta - y\|. \tag{4.3}$$

This *optimisation problem* presents a *closed-form solution*, which is:

$$\hat{\theta} = (X^\top X)^{-1} X^\top y. \tag{4.4}$$

From this, we can clearly see that a **solution** relies on the existence of the inverse $(X^\top X)^{-1}$. This highlights some important *assumptions* and *considerations*:

- **Linearity**: The relationship between the dependent variable and the predictors is linear.
- **Independence**: The residuals are independent.
- **Absence of multicollinearity**: The predictors must not be highly correlated with each other.

The following script shows how to implement a simple linear regression model (see also Figure 4.1) using the Scikit-learn Python library [77]. We use synthetic (i.e., randomly generated) clinical data, assuming a linear relationship between patient age and blood pressure.

```
import numpy as np
import matplotlib.pyplot as plt
import seaborn as sns
from sklearn.linear_model import LinearRegression
from sklearn.model_selection import train_test_split

np.random.seed(42)

# Set publication-style aesthetics
sns.set_theme(style="whitegrid", context="talk")
```

```
# Generate 100 random samples of ages between 30 and 80
ages = np.random.randint(30, 80, size=(100, 1))

# Generate blood pressure labels linearly related to age
↪  data plus noise
blood_pressure = 90 + 0.5 * ages + np.random.randn(100,
↪  1) * 5

# Split the data into training and testing sets
X_train, X_test, y_train, y_test =
↪  train_test_split(ages, blood_pressure,
↪  test_size=0.2, random_state=42)

# Create and fit the linear regression model
lin_reg = LinearRegression()
lin_reg.fit(X_train, y_train)

# Predict blood pressure for visualization
age_range = np.array([[30], [80]])
bp_predictions = lin_reg.predict(age_range)

colours = sns.color_palette("dark", n_colors=3)

# Create the figure
plt.figure(figsize=(10, 6))

plt.scatter(X_train, y_train, color=colours[0],
↪  label='Training Data')
plt.scatter(X_test, y_test, color=colours[2],
↪  label='Test Data', marker='x')
plt.plot(age_range, bp_predictions, color=colours[1],
↪  linewidth=2, label='Regression Line')

# Add title, labels, and grid
plt.xlabel('Age (years)', fontsize=16)
plt.ylabel('Blood Pressure (mmHg)', fontsize=16)
plt.title('Linear Regression: Age vs. Blood Pressure',
↪  fontsize=20, fontweight='bold')
plt.legend(frameon=True, fontsize=14)
plt.grid(True, linestyle='--', alpha=0.6)
sns.despine()

# Show the plot
```

```
plt.tight_layout()
plt.show()
```

The full executable code corresponding to this example is available online and can be accessed, reused, and commented on at: https://github.com/RiverPublishers/Computational-Approaches-in-Biology-and-Medicine/blob/main/Chapter4.ipynb

Figure 4.1: Fitted regression line illustrating the relationship between the two variables under study. The solid red line represents the best-fitting linear model. This visualisation highlights the direction and strength of the association, allowing for assessment of potential trends or deviations from linearity.

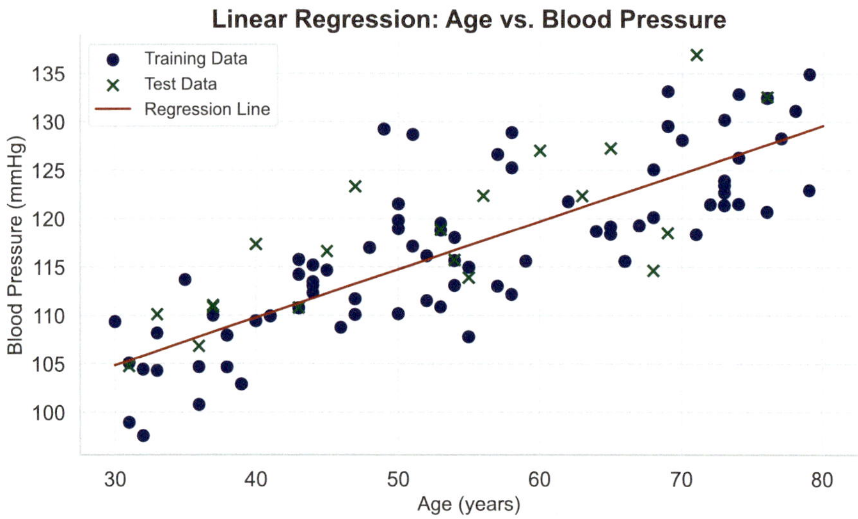

In many biomedical applications, where datasets may have a large number of features relative to the number of samples, overfitting becomes a significant concern. Regularisation techniques add penalty terms to the loss function to discourage overly complex models. Two common forms are *ridge regression* (L2 penalty), which shrinks coefficients smoothly toward zero, and *least absolute shrinkage and selection operator (LASSO) regression* (L1 penalty), which can drive some coefficients exactly to zero, performing *implicit feature selection*. These approaches help improve generalisation in high-dimensional settings.

4.2.3 Logistic regression

Logistic regression (LR) is a model used for *binary classification* tasks, where the output variable y takes on values 0 or 1. Instead of modelling the outcome directly, LR models the *probability* that y equals 1 as a function of the input variables, using a *logit function*. In particular, the model is defined using the sigmoid function:

$$P(y = 1 \mid x) = \frac{1}{1 + \exp\left(-(\theta_0 + \theta_1 x_1 + \cdots + \theta_m x_m)\right)}. \tag{4.5}$$

Compared to linear regression, the *parameters* in the LR model are typically estimated using *maximum likelihood estimation (MLE)*, where the likelihood function takes the form:

$$L(\theta) = \prod_{i=1}^{n} \left[P(y_i = 1 \mid x_i)\right]^{y_i} \left[1 - P(y_i = 1 \mid x_i)\right]^{1-y_i}. \tag{4.6}$$

LR can also be extended to handle *multi-class classification* problems where the *target variable* has more than two categories. This extension is known as *multinomial LR*. There are two common strategies to implement multinomial LR:

- **One-vs-rest**: The classifier trains K binary LR models, each treating one class as the positive class and the rest as the negative class. The final prediction is made based on the class with the highest probability of occurrence.
- **Softmax regression**: Instead of training separate binary classifiers, softmax regression directly models all classes using a single optimisation function, making it more efficient for multi-class problems.

Here, we provide a small code snippet that shows how to implement a simple binary LR model using the sklearn library. For example, we could imagine that the binary target variable y represents a patient's diagnosis of diabetes, and the ultimate goal of the analysis is to model and predict whether a patient has diabetes based on diagnostic measurements.

```
from sklearn.linear_model import LogisticRegression
from sklearn.model_selection import train_test_split

# Load the dataset
...
```

```
# Split the data into training and testing sets
X_train, X_test, y_train, y_test = train_test_split(X,
↪  y, test_size=0.2, random_state=42)

# Create and fit the logistic regression model
log_reg = LogisticRegression()
log_reg.fit(X_train, y_train)

y_pred = log_reg.predict(X_test)
```

The full executable code corresponding to this example is available online and can be accessed, reused, and commented on at: https://github.com/RiverPublishers/Computational-Approaches-in-Biology-and-Medicine/blob/main/Chapter4.ipynb

4.2.4 k-nearest neighbours

The *k-nearest neighbours (k-NN)* algorithm is a *non-parametric*, *instance-based* method used for both *classification* and *regression*.

In the context of classification, k-nearest neighbours (k-NN) predicts the class label of a new instance by identifying the k most similar training examples in the feature space and assigning the majority class among them. The *similarity* between data points is usually measured using a *distance metric*, most commonly the *Euclidean distance*:

$$d(x_i, x_j) = \sqrt{\sum_{l=1}^{D} (x_{i,l} - x_{j,l})^2}, \tag{4.7}$$

where x_i and x_j are two instances in a D-dimensional feature space.

Once distances are computed, the algorithm selects the k-NN and assigns the predicted class label by *majority vote*. That is, the most frequent class among the k neighbours determines the output:

$$\hat{y} = \text{mode}\left(y_i : x_i \in \mathcal{N}_k(x)\right), \tag{4.8}$$

where $\mathcal{N}_k(x)$ denotes the set of k nearest neighbours of the point x, while the function mode is used to calculate the most frequent class label among the selected neighbours.

The choice of k is a *hyperparameter* that significantly influences the model's performance:

- A small k (e.g., $k = 1$) may lead to overfitting and high variance.
- A large k may result in underfitting and high bias.

Note that k-NN does not explicitly train a model; it stores the entire dataset and makes predictions at inference time. Due to this characteristic, it is often referred to as a *lazy learner*. It is computationally expensive during prediction and sensitive to the scale of the data, so preprocessing steps like *normalisation* are important.

Below is a simple implementation of a k-NN for binary classification using the sklearn library.

```
from sklearn.neighbours import KNeighborsClassifier
from sklearn.model_selection import train_test_split

# Load the dataset
...

# Split the data into training and testing sets
X_train, X_test, y_train, y_test = train_test_split(X,
↪  y, test_size=0.2, random_state=42)

# Create and fit the k-NN model (k=5)
knn = KNeighborsClassifier(n_neighbors=5)
knn.fit(X_train, y_train)

# Make predictions on the test set
y_pred = knn.predict(X_test)
```

The full executable code corresponding to this example is available online and can be accessed, reused, and commented on at: https://github.com/RiverPublishers/Computational-Approaches-in-Biology-and-Medicine/blob/main/Chapter4.ipynb

The k-NN algorithm is easy to implement and interpret, making it a useful baseline in many classification tasks. However, it is less suitable for high-dimensional datasets due to the *curse of dimensionality*, which can hinder the meaning of distance-based similarity.

In biomedical applications, k-NN has been used in tasks such as disease classification based on gene expression profiles, patient similarity analysis, and medical image classification.

4.2.5 Decision trees

Decision trees are a fundamental class of *non-parametric supervised learning* algorithms used for both *classification* and *regression* tasks. A decision tree recursively partitions the *feature space* into *distinct regions*, making predictions based on a series of *hierarchical rules*. The model is represented as a *tree-like structure* where each *internal node* corresponds to a *decision rule* based on a feature, each branch represents an outcome of the decision, and each *leaf node* contains a *predicted outcome*.

The recursive partitioning is typically performed using *measures of impurity* or *variance reduction*. In classification, the most common impurity measures include:

- **Gini impurity** (or index):

$$G = 1 - \sum_{k=1}^{K} p_k^2,$$

where p_k is the proportion of class k instances at a given node.

- **Entropy** (an information theory measure, quantifying the average information or uncertainty):

$$H = -\sum_{k=1}^{K} p_k \log_2 p_k.$$

A lower entropy indicates a more homogeneous node.

For regression, trees are typically built using impurity measures that quantify the variance or absolute deviation of the target values within a node.

- **Mean squared error (MSE)**:

$$\text{MSE} = \frac{1}{n}\sum_{i=1}^{n} (y_i - \bar{y})^2,$$

where y_i is the actual value, and $\bar{y}$ is the mean of the target values in the node. MSE penalises larger errors more heavily and leads to splits that minimise the variance within each child node.

- **Mean absolute error (MAE)**:

$$\text{MAE} = \frac{1}{n}\sum_{i=1}^{n} |y_i - \tilde{y}|,$$

where $\tilde{y}$ is the median of the target values in the node. Mean absolute error (MAE) is more robust to outliers and emphasises minimising the average absolute deviation.

A decision tree is constructed using a recursive splitting procedure, which acts as a greedy algorithm. The algorithm seeks to optimise the chosen impurity measure at each split, typically stopping when further splitting no longer provides a meaningful reduction in impurity or when a pre-defined stopping condition is met, such as a minimum number of samples per leaf. Despite their simplicity and interpretability, decision trees are a powerful class of models, and for this reason they are prone to overfitting, especially when they grow too deep. This issue is often mitigated through pruning techniques and early stopping.

Below is a code snippet showing how to build a decision tree for the same problem of diabetes diagnosis prediction described above in the LR paragraph:

```
from sklearn.tree import DecisionTreeClassifier
from sklearn.model_selection import train_test_split

# Load the dataset
...

# Split the data into training and testing sets
X_train, X_test, y_train, y_test = train_test_split(X,
↪  y, test_size=0.2, random_state=42)

# Create and fit the decision tree model:
tree = DecisionTreeClassifier()
tree.fit(X_train, y_train)

y_pred = tree.predict(X_test)
```

The full executable code corresponding to this example is available online and can be accessed, reused, and commented on at: https://github.com/RiverPublishers/Computational-Approaches-in-Biology-and-Medicine/blob/main/Chapter4.ipynb

4.2.6 Ensemble methods

Ensemble methods are powerful techniques that combine multiple base models, rather than relying on a single model (e.g., a single decision tree), to improve predictive performance and robustness. Ensemble methods leverage the diversity among individual learners to reduce variance, bias, or both.

The two main categories of ensemble methods are:

- **Bagging** (bootstrap aggregating): This technique trains multiple instances of the *same model* on *different subsets* of the *training set*, sampled with replacement. The final prediction is obtained by averaging predictions in regression tasks or by majority voting in classification tasks. A well-known family of such models is *random forest (RF)s*, which builds *multiple decision trees* and averages their predictions to reduce *overfitting*.
- **Boosting**: Unlike bagging, boosting sequentially trains *weak learners*, where *each model corrects* the *mistakes* of its *predecessor*. Models in boosting assign *higher weights* to *misclassified examples*, thereby forcing subsequent models to focus on more challenging cases. Popular boosting methods include:
    - **Adaptive boosting (AdaBoost)**: In this method, models are trained iteratively, and their predictions are combined using a weighted sum.
    - **Gradient boosting**: Instead of reweighting observations, gradient boosting optimises a loss function by sequentially training models to correct the residual errors of previous models. This method is utilised in highly popular computational frameworks, such as extreme gradient boosting (XGBoost), light gradient boosting machine (LightGBM), and categorical gradient boosting (Cat- Boost).

Here is a short code snippet implementing a Random rorest (RF) model, using the sklearn library. We can see that the code is actually very similar to the one used for the decision tree model.

```
from sklearn.ensemble import RandomForestClassifier
from sklearn.model_selection import train_test_split

# Load the dataset
...

# Split the data into training and testing sets
X_train, X_test, y_train, y_test = train_test_split(X,
 ↪  y, test_size=0.2, random_state=42)

# Create and fit the random forest model
forest = RandomForestClassifier()
forest.fit(X_train, y_train)

y_pred = forest.predict(X_test)
```

The full executable code corresponding to this example is available online and can be accessed, reused, and commented on at: https://github.com/RiverPublishers/Computational-Approaches-in-Biology-and-Medicine/blob/main/Chapter4.ipynb

4.2.7 Neural networks

Neural networks (NNs), also known as *multilayer perceptron (MLP)*, are a class of *highly flexible ML models* capable of capturing complex *non-linear relationships* between inputs and outputs. They do so by composing *multiple layers* of learned transformations. Each layer performs a *linear transformation* of the input, followed by the application of a *nonlinear activation function*, enabling the network to model intricate and hierarchical patterns in data.

Modern Neural networks (NNs) have achieved *state-of-the-art performance* in a wide range of domains, including image recognition, natural language understanding, and genomics. However, they typically require *large amounts of labelled training data*, substantial *computational resources*, and careful design choices, such as appropriate *regularisation strategies* to prevent overfitting. In biomedical applications, NNs have been used for tasks such as *medical image classification*, *gene expression pattern analysis*, and *predictive modelling of disease progression* or *patient outcomes*. Despite their power, NNs are often considered *black-box models*, and their lack of interpretability can be a challenge in clinical contexts where explainability is crucial.

A detailed study of NNs, particularly their architectures, training algorithms, and interpretability methods, is beyond the scope of this chapter. Readers interested in deep learning are encouraged to consult dedicated resources focusing on NN theory and applications.

4.3 Unsupervised Learning

Unlike supervised learning, where models learn from input-output pairs, *unsupervised learning* algorithms work with *raw, unlabeled data* to find *meaningful groupings* or *patterns*. The two primary applications of the unsupervised learning paradigm in *data analysis* are dimensionality *reduction* and *clustering*. In recent years, unsupervised learning has also played a central role in the development of *generative models*, such as those used in generative artificial intelligence (AI). However, the study of generative models falls outside the scope of this chapter.

4.3.1 Clustering

Clustering is a fundamental technique in *unsupervised learning* that groups similar data points based on *intrinsic structure* in the data, without the need for labelled outcomes. It is widely used in data exploration and pattern discovery. The goal is to identify *natural groupings or clusters* where points within the same cluster are more similar to each other than to points in different clusters.

The most commonly used clustering algorithms include:

- **k-means clustering**: A widely used partition-based algorithm that divides the data into K *disjoint clusters* by minimising the *within-cluster variance* (sum of squared distances between points and their assigned cluster centroids). The algorithm iteratively assigns each point to the nearest cluster centroid and then updates the centroids until convergence. The objective function is:

$$J = \sum_{i=1}^{K} \sum_{x_j \in C_i} |x_j - \mu_i|^2,$$

  where μ_i is the centroid of cluster C_i.
  Assumptions:
    - The number of clusters K is known and fixed in advance.
    - Clusters are roughly spherical and of similar size.
    - It uses *Euclidean distance*, so features should be on the same scale.
    - Sensitive to outliers and initialisation.

- **Hierarchical clustering**: This method builds a nested hierarchy of clusters using either an *agglomerative* (bottom-up) or *divisive* (top-down) approach. The output is a *dendrogram* that can be cut at different levels to produce the desired number of clusters.
  Assumptions:
    - No need to pre-specify the number of clusters.
    - Distance metric and linkage criteria (e.g., average, complete, single) affect the shape of clusters.
    - Sensitive to noise and outliers.

- **Density-based spatial clustering of applications with noise (DBSCAN)**: This algorithm groups together points that are densely packed and separates low-density regions as outliers. It does not require specifying the number of clusters and can discover clusters of arbitrary shape.
  Assumptions:

- Clusters are dense regions separated by low-density areas.
- Two hyperparameters: eps (radius) and min_samples (minimum points per cluster).
- It struggles in datasets with varying density.

- **Gaussian mixture model (GMM)**: A probabilistic model that assumes the data are generated from a mixture of Gaussian distributions. Each point is assigned a probability of belonging to each cluster, allowing for soft (fuzzy) assignments and elliptical cluster shapes.
  Assumptions:
  - Data are generated from a mixture of Gaussian distributions.
  - Clusters may have different sizes and covariance structures.
  - Requires the number of components (clusters) to be defined *a priori*.
  - Sensitive to initialisation; typically fitted using the expectation–maximisation (EM) algorithm.

Choosing the *right clustering algorithm* depends on the structure of the dataset, noise levels, the expected shape of clusters, and computational constraints. For instance, since *k-means* relies on Euclidean distances and assumes isotropic clusters, it can struggle in *high-dimensional spaces* due to the *curse of dimensionality*. This issue can be mitigated by applying *dimensionality reduction* techniques, such as *Principal component analysis (PCA)*, before clustering.

On the other hand, *hierarchical clustering* provides a global view of data structure through a tree-based representation, making it useful for exploratory analysis. *Density-based spatial clustering of applications with noise (DBSCAN)* is robust to noise and can detect clusters of arbitrary shape, but may underperform when clusters have varying densities. *Gaussian mixture model (GMM)s* offer flexibility in modelling elliptical clusters but require careful tuning and computational resources.

One application of the k-means algorithm could be, for example, to cluster patients based on common features. The Python snippet below implements the k-means algorithm.

```
from sklearn.cluster import KMeans
from sklearn import preprocessing

# Load the dataset
...

# Normalise the data
X_normalized = preprocessing.normalize(X)
```

```
# Create and fit K-means model
kmeans = KMeans(n_clusters = 3, random_state = 42,
↪   n_init='auto')
kmeans.fit(X_normalized)

# Get the cluster centroids and the label for each
↪   datapoint
cluster_labels = kmeans.labels_
cluster_centroids = kmeans.cluster_centers_
```

The full executable code corresponding to this example is available online and can be accessed, reused, and commented on at: https://github.com/RiverPublishers/Computational-Approaches-in-Biology-and-Medicine/blob/main/Chapter4.ipynb

4.3.2 Dimensionality reduction

Dimensionality reduction refers to a class of techniques used to reduce the number of input variables (features) in a dataset while preserving its essential structure and underlying patterns. The main objective is to transform high-dimensional data into a more compact representation that retains the most relevant information for downstream tasks such as visualisation, clustering, or classification.

This transformation is typically achieved by learning a new set of features, also known as *latent variables* or *components*, that capture the variability or structure of the original data. Dimensionality reduction can be broadly categorised into:

- **Linear methods**, which assume that the data lies on or near a linear subspace of the high-dimensional feature space.
- **Nonlinear methods**, which aim to capture more complex, curved manifolds embedded in high-dimensional space.

Dimensionality reduction plays a crucial role in mitigating the *curse of dimensionality*, which refers to a set of challenges that arise as the number of features grows:

- The *volume* of the feature space increases exponentially, making data points sparser and harder to analyse.

- Algorithms that rely on *distance metrics* (e.g., k-NN, clustering) become less effective.
- The number of samples required to estimate statistical properties reliably also increases, amplifying the risk of *overfitting* and noise sensitivity.

By projecting the data into a lower-dimensional space, dimensionality reduction improves model performance, enhances interpretability, and enables efficient visualisation.

- **PCA**: A classical linear technique that identifies the directions (principal components) along which the variance in the data is maximised [78]. Formally, PCA solves an eigenvalue problem on the covariance matrix of the data. The first principal component captures the direction of maximum variance, the second captures the next highest variance orthogonal to the first, and so on. Given a data matrix $\boldsymbol{X} \in \mathbb{R}^{N \times D}$, PCA seeks to find a transformation matrix $\boldsymbol{W} \in \mathbb{R}^{D \times K}$ such that:
$$\boldsymbol{Z} = \boldsymbol{X}\boldsymbol{W},$$
where where $\boldsymbol{Z} \in \mathbb{R}^{N \times K}$ is the projected data in the reduced K-dimensional space. PCA is sensitive to the scale of the features, so standardisation (e.g., z-score normalisation) is recommended before applying it.
- **t-distributed stochastic neighbour embedding (t-SNE)**: A nonlinear technique designed for visualising high-dimensional data in 2 or 3 dimensions [79]. Unlike PCA, t-distributed stochastic neighbour embedding (t-SNE) focuses on preserving the *local structure* of the data by modelling the pairwise similarities between data points. In high dimensions, similarities are computed using a Gaussian kernel, whereas in lower-dimensional spaces, a Student's t-distribution is employed. The algorithm minimises the divergence between these distributions using a cost function based on Kullback–Leibler divergence. t-SNE is widely used for exploring complex data (e.g., scRNA-seq) but is computationally expensive and not well-suited for general-purpose dimensionality reduction pipelines.
- **Uniform manifold approximation and projection (UMAP)**: A nonlinear dimensionality reduction method that, like t-SNE, is primarily used for visualising complex high-dimensional data in two or three dimensions [80, 81]. Uniform manifold approximation and projection (UMAP) is based on principles from manifold theory and topological data analysis, constructing a weighted graph to represent local relationships between data points in high-dimensional space and optimising a low-dimensional embedding that preserves both *local and global structure*. Compared to t-SNE, UMAP is typically faster, scales better to large datasets, and tends to maintain more of the overall data geometry, making it suitable for both exploratory visualisation and as a preprocessing step for supervised and unsupervised tasks.

Below is a Python snippet implementing PCA using the sklearn library:

```
from sklearn.decomposition import PCA
from sklearn.preprocessing import StandardScaler
```

```
# Load the dataset
...

# Standardise features (important before PCA)
X_scaled = StandardScaler().fit_transform(X)

# Apply PCA to reduce to 2 dimensions
pca = PCA(n_components=2)
X_pca = pca.fit_transform(X_scaled)
```

The full executable code corresponding to this example is available online and can be accessed, reused, and commented on at: https://github.com/RiverPublishers/Computational-Approaches-in-Biology-and-Medicine/blob/main/Chapter4.ipynb

In practice, PCA is often used as a preprocessing step before clustering, visualisation, or supervised learning. While PCA provides interpretable axes of variance, it assumes that these relationships are linear. It may not perform well when the data lies on a nonlinear manifold, where methods such as t-SNE, UMAP, or autoencoders may be more suitable.

4.4 Feature Selection

Biomedical datasets often contain a large number of features, many of which may be **noisy**, *irrelevant*, or *redundant*. This high dimensionality can hinder model performance, lead to overfitting, and reduce interpretability. *Feature selection* refers to the process of identifying the most relevant variables in a dataset for a given predictive task, with the goal of improving *generalisation*, *computational efficiency*, and *model transparency* [82].

Feature selection methods can be broadly categorised into three classes:

- **Filter methods**: These select features based on univariate statistical tests or intrinsic properties of the data, independently of any specific ML model. Common techniques include:
    - *t-test* or *ANOVA* for continuous features in classification tasks.
    - *Chi-squared test* for categorical features.
    - *Mutual information* for quantifying nonlinear associations between features and target variables.

Filter methods are computationally efficient and suitable as a preprocessing step, but they do not account for feature interactions.

- **Wrapper methods**: These approaches evaluate subsets of features by training and validating a predictive model, thus directly optimising performance. A common example is *recursive feature elimination (RFE)*, which recursively removes the least important features based on model coefficients or performance metrics. While often more accurate, wrapper methods are computationally expensive and can overfit if not carefully cross-validated.
- **Embedded methods**: These perform feature selection as part of the model training process. Examples include:

    - **Least absolute shrinkage and selection operator (LASSO)**, which applies L1 regularisation to zero out irrelevant features.
    - **Tree-based models** (e.g., RFs), which provide feature importance scores based on impurity reduction.

Embedded methods offer a balance between computational efficiency and performance by leveraging model-specific inductive biases.

Choosing an appropriate feature selection strategy depends on the nature of the data, the learning task, the model being used, and the trade-off between accuracy and interpretability. In clinical and biomedical contexts, feature selection helps reduce the *curse of dimensionality*. It supports the discovery of *interpretable biomarkers* and *risk factors* that can inform diagnosis, prognosis, or treatment decisions.

Below is a single Python script that integrates all three feature selection strategies (i.e., filter, wrapper, and embedded) using the breast_cancer dataset from scikit-learn.

```
import numpy as np
from sklearn.datasets import load_breast_cancer
from sklearn.feature_selection import SelectKBest,
↪  f_classif, RFE
from sklearn.linear_model import LogisticRegression
from sklearn.preprocessing import StandardScaler

# Load and standardise data
X, y = load_breast_cancer(return_X_y=True)
feature_names = load_breast_cancer().feature_names
X = StandardScaler().fit_transform(X)
```

```
# Initialise the model (used for wrapper and embedded
↪  methods)
model = LogisticRegression(penalty='l1',
↪  solver='liblinear', C=0.1, max_iter=1000)

# 1. Filter method: SelectKBest (ANOVA F-test)
# Use this when you want to remove irrelevant features
↪  using univariate tests quickly.
filter_selector = SelectKBest(score_func=f_classif,
↪  k=10)
X_filter = filter_selector.fit_transform(X, y)
filter_selected =
↪  filter_selector.get_support(indices=True)

# 2. Wrapper method: Recursive Feature Elimination (RFE)
# Use RFE when you want to optimise model performance
↪  while reducing dimensionality.
rfe_selector =
↪  RFE(estimator=LogisticRegression(max_iter=1000),
↪  n_features_to_select=10)
X_rfe = rfe_selector.fit_transform(X, y)
rfe_selected = rfe_selector.get_support(indices=True)

# 3. Embedded method: LASSO (L1 regularisation)
# Use LASSO when you want embedded selection that is
↪  fast, interpretable, and robust to correlated
↪  features.
model.fit(X, y)
lasso_selected = np.where(model.coef_[0] != 0)[0]

# Display selected feature names for each method
def print_selected(name, indices):
print(f"\n{name} Selected Features ({len(indices)}):")
for i in indices:
print(f"- {feature_names[i]}")

print_selected("Filter (SelectKBest)", filter_selected)
print_selected("Wrapper (RFE)", rfe_selected)
print_selected("Embedded (LASSO)", lasso_selected)
```

The full executable code corresponding to this example is available online and can be accessed, reused, and commented on at: https://github.com/RiverPublishers/Computational-Approaches-in-Biology-and-Medicine/blob/main/Chapter4.ipynb

4.5 Additional Foundations for Predictive Modelling

In this section, we take a deeper look at often-overlooked but critical aspects of predictive modelling. We explore how to define and evaluate performance against appropriate null models, how to systematically choose and validate models, and how to balance complexity with interpretability and reproducibility, particularly in the context of real-world biomedical data. Each subsection is designed to reinforce sound modelling practices and highlight their importance in building robust, transparent, and clinically applicable predictive models.

4.5.1 Baselines, null models, and random guessing

Every predictive model must be evaluated in context. Before deploying complex ML algorithms, it is essential to establish a simple *reference point* to judge performance. This is typically done through a *baseline model*. Without this comparison, evaluation metrics can appear deceptively high, even when the model fails to learn meaningful patterns. A *baseline model* is an intentionally simple model or prediction strategy used as a *reference point* to evaluate the performance of more complex models. It reflects the minimal level of performance that one could reasonably expect without leveraging any domain knowledge or sophisticated modelling. Rather than being a benchmark to "beat", a good baseline helps *contextualise model performance*: it answers the question, *Is the model extracting signal, or just exploiting artefacts or imbalances in the data?* In biomedical applications—where interpretability and safety are paramount—understanding what a naive model would achieve is essential for robust evaluation. Baseline models also help answer: *Is our model learning anything useful? Would a naive approach achieve similar results? Is the observed performance better than random or trivial predictions?*

In biomedical applications, where interpretability and safety are paramount, understanding what a naive model would achieve is essential for robust evaluation.

Note that the terms *baseline model* and *null model* are often used interchangeably, While the terms are sometimes used interchangeably in informal discussions, they serve different purposes in rigorous modelling workflows. Table 4.1 summarises the main differences between these models, which are foundational concepts in evaluating predictive performance. While both serve as reference points, baseline models are practical tools used during model development to evaluate whether more complex approaches offer substantial

Table 4.1: Comparison between baseline models and null models in biomedical predictive modelling.

Aspect	Baseline model	Null model
Definition	A simple, often heuristic model used to provide a minimal level of expected performance in a given task.	A model that assumes no relationship between input features and outcomes. It represents the hypothesis of no signal.
Purpose	To serve as a practical reference for comparing more complex models.	To test whether the observed model performance could be due to chance.
Philosophical basis	Pragmatic: "How well can we do without any real modelling effort?"	Statistical: "Could this result arise if there were no real association?"
Use case	Model development and evaluation	Hypothesis testing and permutation testing
Example	Predict majority class (Zero-R), mean of outcomes, last value in time series, linear regression with intercept only	Permuted-label model, randomised features, Kaplan–Meier for survival, white-noise predictors
Output	Performance metrics from a simple strategy on real data	Null distribution of performance metrics under no association
Interpretation	"Is our model better than a trivial solution?"	"Is our model significantly better than random?"

improvements over naive strategies. In contrast, null models are grounded in statistical inference. They are primarily used to test whether observed performance could plausibly arise under the assumption of no relationship between features and outcomes. In practice, null models are underused in applied ML, partly due to the computational cost of generating null distributions (e.g., via permutation testing) and the lack of built-in support in standard libraries. However, they remain a gold standard for validating model significance. However, understanding and correctly applying both is essential for robust and interpretable biomedical modelling. In practice, use a baseline model to set expectations: *Can a simple strategy achieve good results?* If so, complex models must offer clear advantages (e.g., better generalisation, interpretability). Use a null model to validate discoveries: *Is the model's performance statistically meaningful, or could it have arisen by chance?*

Random guessing:

In a balanced binary classification task, randomly assigning labels will yield an expected accuracy of 50%, which is the weakest possible baseline. For imbalanced classes, random guessing tends to favour the majority class. While this is an intentionally weak baseline, it acts as a *sanity check*: if your model performs below or near this level, it is not learning anything meaningful.

Zero-R (zero rule classifier):

The Zero-R model always predicts the majority class (classification) or the mean value (regression), regardless of input features. While naive, Zero-R often performs surprisingly well in imbalanced datasets and serves as a practical reference.

Example: In a cancer detection dataset where 90% of samples are healthy, Zero-R achieves 90% accuracy by always predicting "healthy". However, it fails to identify a single cancer case, which is an unacceptable outcome in a clinical setting.

Task-specific nulls:

Baseline choice should reflect the domain and task:

- **Time series**: A common null model is the "last value" (i.e., predicting the most recent observed value at each timestep).
- **Survival analysis**: The Kaplan–Meier estimator serves as a non-parametric reference for survival probabilities over time.
- **Omics data**: Nulls may involve permuting sample labels, shuffling gene expression profiles, or replacing structured features with noise while preserving the label distribution.

4.5.2 Sanity checks and Occam's razor

Just because a model runs, and even achieves high performance, does not mean it is valid or useful. In real-world modelling, especially in biomedical applications, simple *sanity checks* are critical to detect issues such as data leakage, overfitting, or spurious correlations.

Recommended *sanity checks*:

- **Label shuffling:** Randomise the labels and retrain the model. Performance should drop to chance levels or baseline. If not, this may indicate data leakage, overfitting, or reliance on irrelevant patterns.

- **Random features:** Replace input features with noise or random values. A significant drop in performance is expected to follow. If the model still performs well, it may be memorising sample order, exploiting feature encoding artefacts, or leveraging hidden leakage.
- **Simple model comparison:** Benchmark your complex model against a baseline model, such as LR or decision trees. If the more complex model does not yield substantially better performance, its additional complexity may be unjustified.

These sanity checks ensure that model performance reflects genuine signal extraction rather than artefacts, bias, or noise. This brings us to *Occam's Razor*, a foundational principle in science and statistical modelling [83]. It suggests that, when two or more models perform similarly, the *simpler* one should be preferred. Simpler models are generally easier to interpret, faster to train, and less prone to overfitting.

In biomedical contexts, *simplicity* often is linked to *interpretability*, which is essential for clinical validation, regulatory approval, and physician trust. A slightly less accurate, but more transparent, model may be preferable in practice.

4.5.3 Cross-validation and statistical reliability

In biomedical research, where datasets are often small, noisy, or imbalanced, evaluating a model's ability to generalise is critical. *CV* provides a robust framework for estimating performance on unseen data while mitigating overfitting [84, 85]. Unlike a fixed train/test split, CV repeatedly partitions the dataset into *training and validation subsets*, trains the model, and averages the performance metric across runs. This yields more reliable performance estimates, especially when data are scarce.

Common CV strategies include:

- **k-fold CV**: The dataset is split into k equal-sized folds (typical choice are $k = 5$ or 10 based on the number of samples). The model is trained on $k - 1$ folds and validated on the remaining fold. This process is repeated k times, each time using a different fold as the validation set. The overall performance is the average across all k runs. Larger k reduces bias in performance estimation but increases computational cost and variance.
- **Stratified k-fold CV**: It ensures that the proportion of classes (e.g., disease vs. healthy) is preserved in each fold. This is particularly important for imbalanced classification tasks, which are common in clinical datasets.

- **Leave-one-out CV (LOO-CV)**: A special and extreme case where $k = n$, where n is the number of samples. Each instance is used once as the validation set. While this provides nearly unbiased estimates for small datasets, it is computationally expensive.
- **Nested CV**: It is used when both hyperparameter tuning and performance estimation are required. The *inner loop* performs model selection (e.g., choosing regularisation strength), while the *outer loop* evaluates generalisation.
  A nested CV avoids optimistic bias that can occur if the same data are used for both model tuning and final evaluation. It is considered best practice for comparing models in research settings.

Permutation testing:

In addition to CV, *permutation tests* offer a way to assess whether a model's performance is statistically significant. They build a *null distribution* of performance scores under the assumption that there is no relationship between the features and the outcome. To do so, you can follow these four steps:

1. Randomly shuffle the labels.
2. Train the model and compute a performance metric (e.g., accuracy).
3. Repeat this process many times (e.g., 1000 iterations).
4. Compare the original (unpermuted) performance to the null distribution.

The *p-value* is the proportion of permuted scores that are equal to or better than the original score. This provides a formal answer to the question: *Could this performance have occurred by chance?*

Note: Permutation tests are computationally intensive but valuable for validating model performance, especially in high-dimensional, low-sample biomedical datasets.

4.5.4 Hyperparameter tuning and model selection

In ML, *hyperparameters* are configuration settings that control the training process of a model but are not learned from the data itself [86]. They govern aspects such as model complexity, regularisation strength, learning rate, the structure of a NN, or the maximum depth of decision trees. This distinguishes them from model *parameters* (e.g., regression coefficients), which are directly estimated during training. Common examples of hyperparameters include:

- Learning rate (in gradient-based methods)
- Maximum tree depth (for decision trees)
- Number of estimators (in ensembles such as RF or gradient boosting)

- Regularisation strength (e.g., L1 or L2 penalty)
- Number of hidden layers or units (in NNs).

Selecting appropriate hyperparameters is critical for achieving optimal model performance.

Several strategies are commonly used:

- **Random search**: Randomly samples configurations from the hyperparameter space. Surprisingly effective in practice, especially when only a few hyperparameters dominate performance. However, it may miss optimal regions [86].
- **Grid search**: This performs an exhaustive search over a predefined set of hyperparameter combinations. While conceptually simple, it becomes inefficient and computationally expensive as the number of hyperparameters increases (the "curse of dimensionality" in hyperparameter space).
- **Bayesian optimisation**: A more efficient global optimisation approach that models the performance landscape using a surrogate function or model (e.g., a Gaussian process) [87]. It balances *exploration* (trying uncertain regions) and *exploitation* (focusing on promising areas). This method is particularly useful when evaluations are expensive or data are limited.

In biomedical ML, where datasets are often small and sensitive to overfitting, *nested CV* is strongly recommended for model selection. This technique uses:

- An *inner loop* to perform hyperparameter tuning.
- An *outer loop* to evaluate generalisation performance.

Nested CV avoids **data leakage**, which occurs when the same data is used for both model selection and evaluation. This is especially important when working with repeated measures, patient-level time series, or multiple samples from the same patient.

Key rule: Never tune hyperparameters on the test set. Doing so invalidates performance estimates.

Clinical example: In patient classification tasks, if samples from the same patient appear in both training and validation folds, the model may learn individual signatures rather than generalisable disease features—leading to inflated performance.

As a *golden rule*, select the model that best balances *predictive performance*, *complexity*, and *interpretability*. In biomedical contexts, a slightly less accurate but more interpretable model may be preferred for clinical deployment.

Table 4.2: Examples of common ML models and their associated inductive biases. Each model encodes assumptions about the structure of the data, which influence its ability to generalise. Selecting a model whose bias aligns with the underlying data can significantly improve performance and interpretability.

Model type	Inductive bias
Logistic regression	Relationships are linear and additive
Decision trees	Data can be partitioned by axis-aligned thresholds
k-NN	Nearby samples have similar labels
NNs	Hierarchical, nonlinear feature interactions

4.5.5 Inductive bias and bias–variance trade-off

All learning algorithms make implicit or explicit assumptions about how the input features relate to the output. These assumptions, whether explicit or implicit, are known as the model's *inductive bias* [88]. Without such biases, generalisation from finite datasets would be impossible.

Different model families exhibit different inductive biases, which guide their learning behaviour. Table 4.2 shows examples of common models and their associated assumptions. Choosing a model appropriate to the task requires understanding these assumptions, as well as the structure underlying the data.

In biomedical applications, aligning the inductive bias of the model with domain knowledge can substantially improve both predictive performance and interpretability. For example:

- **Gene expression data** often benefits from *sparsity-inducing models*, such as LASSO, which select only the most informative genes.
- **Longitudinal studies** benefit from models that incorporate *temporal structure*, such as autoregressive models or time-aware NNs.
- **Genomic sequence data** is often modelled with *convolutional NNs* or *transformers*, which can learn hierarchical and positional patterns in the input sequence.

The bias–variance trade-off:

A trade-off exists between bias and variance, governing model performance [89]. A central challenge in predictive modelling is balancing *bias* and *variance*:

- **High-bias models** (e.g., linear regression) are simple and stable but may underfit the data, failing to capture meaningful patterns.
- **High-variance models** (e.g., deep NNs) are highly flexible and can overfit noisy training data, especially when sample sizes are small.

This trade-off is captured by the decomposition of the expected prediction error, and the *total error* is given by the following relation:

$$\text{Total error} = \text{Bias}^2 + \text{Variance} + \text{Irreducible error},$$

where the irreducible error reflects the inherent noise in the data and cannot be reduced by any model.

Thus, *our goal* is to minimise the total error by finding an optimal balance between model complexity and generalisation capacity. This balance is generally achieved through *regularisation* (e.g., L1/L2 penalties), model selection (e.g., choosing simpler architectures or shallower trees), and data augmentation.

In biomedical research, where datasets are often high-dimensional and sample-limited, controlling variance is especially important. In such settings, simpler models may outperform complex ones, not because they capture more intricate patterns, but because they are more robust to noise and less prone to overfitting. When interpretability is also required (as in clinical decision support), high-bias, low-variance models are often preferred.

4.5.6 Evaluation metrics

In biomedical applications, evaluating the performance of an ML model requires more than simply reporting its overall accuracy. Many clinical datasets are imbalanced, involve high-risk decisions, and present asymmetric costs for false positives and false negatives. Choosing the right evaluation metric depends on both the *task type* (i.e., classification or regression) and the *clinical context* in which the model is applied.

Table 4.3: Confusion matrix for a binary classification task.

	Predicted positive	Predicted negative
Actual positive	True positive (TP)	False negative (FN)
Actual negative	False positive (FP)	True negative (TN)

Classification tasks:

In classification, the goal is to assign a new observation to one of several discrete categories [90]. The output is a *categorical variable* (e.g., disease vs. healthy). The foundation of most classification metrics is the *confusion matrix*, which categorises predictions as true or false, positive or negative (Table 4.3). To better understand the model performance of a classification model, we start with the following four fundamental quantities.

- True positive (TP): The model correctly predicts the presence of the condition (e.g., correctly identifies a patient with disease).
- True negative (TN): The model correctly predicts the absence of the condition (e.g., correctly identifies a healthy patient).
- False positive (FP): The model incorrectly predicts the presence of the condition (e.g., falsely diagnoses a healthy patient as diseased).
- False negative (FN): The model fails to detect the condition (e.g., incorrectly labels a diseased patient as healthy).

From these quantities, we derive a suite of evaluation metrics, shown in Table 4.4.

In clinical applications, especially those involving rare diseases, accuracy can be misleading. For instance, in a dataset where only 1% of patients have a condition, a model that predicts"healthy" for every patient achieves 99% accuracy, despite failing to detect any true cases. In such settings:

- **Sensitivity** is crucial when failing to detect a true positive (e.g., missing a disease), as it carries serious consequences.
- **Precision** becomes important when false positives lead to costly or invasive follow-up procedures.
- The **F1 score** balances precision and recall and is often used when both types of error are clinically relevant.

Table 4.4: Evaluation metrics for classification problems.

Metric	Formula	Interpretation
Accuracy	$\frac{TP+TN}{TP+TN+FP+FN}$	Overall proportion of correct predictions.
Sensitivity (recall, true positive rate)	$\frac{TP}{TP+FN}$	Ability to correctly identify positive cases (e.g., detecting patients with disease).
Specificity (true negative rate)	$\frac{TN}{TN+FP}$	Ability to correctly identify negative cases (e.g., correctly classifying healthy patients).
Positive predictive value (PPV)	$\frac{TP}{TP+FP}$	Proportion of predicted positives that are truly positive.
Negative predictive value	$\frac{TN}{TN+FN}$	Proportion of predicted negatives that are truly negative.
F1 score	$2 \times \frac{\text{Precision} \times \text{Recall}}{\text{Precision}+\text{Recall}}$	Harmonic mean of precision and recall; it balances both types of error.
Receiver operating characteristic area under the curve (ROC-AUC)	–	It evaluates the trade-off between sensitivity and specificity.
Precision–recall area under the curve (PR-AUC)	–	It is more informative for imbalanced datasets.
Calibration	–	It measures how well predicted probabilities reflect actual outcome frequencies.

- **Precision–recall area under the curve (PR-AUC)** is often preferred over receiver operating characteristic area under the curve (ROCAUC) in imbalanced datasets, as it focuses on the positive class.
- **Calibration** is essential in risk prediction models, ensuring that predicted probabilities are interpretable and actionable.

Regression tasks:

In regression, the output is a continuous variable (e.g., blood pressure, age, survival time). Evaluation focuses on how closely the model's predictions align with the true values. Table 4.5 summarises the most common regression metrics.

Among these, MAE is often the most interpretable, as it directly reflects the average prediction error in the same units as the clinical outcome. MSE and root mean squared error (RMSE) give more weight to large errors, which may be more appropriate when large deviations have serious consequences (e.g., incorrect drug dosage). The R^2 score provides a global measure of model fit, but it may be misleading in noisy or high-dimensional biomedical datasets.

Table 4.5: Evaluation metrics for regression problems.

Metric	Formula	Interpretation
MAE	$\frac{1}{n}\sum_{i=1}^{n} \lvert y_i - \hat{y}_i \rvert$	Average magnitude of prediction errors; interpretable in original units.
MSE	$\frac{1}{n}\sum_{i=1}^{n} (y_i - \hat{y}_i)^2$	It penalises large errors more heavily; sensitive to outliers.
Root mean squared error (RMSE)	$\sqrt{\text{MSE}}$	Same units as target variable; commonly reported.
R^2 (coefficient of determination)	$1 - \frac{\sum(y_i - \hat{y}_i)^2}{\sum(y_i - \bar{y})^2}$	Proportion of variance explained by the model; values closer to 1 indicates better fit.

Best practice:

No single metric can fully capture model quality. For a complete assessment, it is advisable to report multiple metrics and consider their implications in the specific biomedical context.

4.5.7 Imbalanced data

Class imbalance, where one outcome class is far more frequent than the other, is one of the most common and challenging issues in biomedical ML. It is particularly prevalent in clinical datasets where the event of interest is rare. For example:

- Rare diseases may affect only 1 patient out of 1000.
- Adverse drug reactions may occur in fewer than 5% of treated patients.
- Treatment failure or complications may be rare in well-controlled clinical cohorts.

Why does imbalance matter?

In imbalanced datasets, most ML algorithms are biased toward the majority class, as they optimise for overall accuracy. This often results in models that perform well on the dominant class but fail to detect the minority class, which is typically the clinically important one.

Note that misclassification costs are asymmetric (e.g., false-negative cancer diagnoses). For instance, in a sepsis prediction model where only 5% of intensive care unit (ICU) patients develop sepsis, a model that always predicts "no sepsis" would achieve 95% accuracy, yet fail to identify a single true case of sepsis. Similarly, in cancer screening studies with <1% disease prevalence, a model reporting 99% accuracy may still have poor positive predictive value (PPV). In these cases, metrics like *sensitivity*, *specificity*, and *Positive predictive value (PPV)* are far more relevant than overall accuracy.

Strategies to handle imbalanced data:

Several strategies have been developed to mitigate class imbalance. These can be broadly grouped into three categories:

1. **Data-level approaches**: They modify the distribution of the training data.

    - **Oversampling**: It increases the number of minority class examples by duplication or synthetic data generation (e.g., synthetic minority oversampling technique (SMOTE)).
    - **Undersampling**: This reduces the number of majority class examples to balance class proportions.
    - **Hybrid methods**: They combine oversampling and undersampling for better balance.

    Note: Resampling should only be applied to the training set, not the validation or test sets, to avoid inflated performance estimates.

2. **Algorithm-level approaches**: They modify the learning process to account for imbalance.

    - **Cost-sensitive learning**: This assigns higher penalties to errors on the minority class.
    - **Class weighting**: It uses class-specific weights in the loss function (e.g., in LR, NNs).
    - **Focal loss**: This adjusts the loss function to focus more on difficult-to-classify samples.

3. **Model-level approaches**: They use model architectures or ensemble methods that are robust to imbalance.

    - **Balanced RF** and **Boosting variants**: They incorporate internal mechanisms for handling class imbalance.
    - **Threshold tuning**: This adjusts the decision threshold to optimise metrics like sensitivity, specificity, or F1-score based on clinical priorities.

Clinical Example

Consider an ML model designed to predict adverse cardiac events after surgery, which occur in only 3% of patients. A model that ignores class imbalance may achieve high accuracy by simply predicting "no event" for all patients; however, this approach would miss critical cases. Applying resampling, class-weighted losses, or threshold tuning can significantly enhance the detection of these rare but high-impact events while maintaining control over false alarm rates.

4.5.8 Reinforcement learning in biomedicine

RL is an ML paradigm that focuses on learning optimal *decision-making policies* through trial-and-error interactions with an environment. Unlike supervised learning, which learns from labelled input–output pairs, RL agents learn by receiving *rewards* for their actions over time, enabling them to optimise behaviour in sequential, uncertain settings.

While still relatively rare in clinical practice, RL has shown significant promise for a range of biomedical applications, including:

- Personalised and adaptive treatment strategies.
- Sequential decision-making (e.g., multi-step care plans).
- Treatment timing and dosing optimisation.
- Dynamic resource allocation in critical care (e.g., Intensive care unit (ICU) management).

RL frames the problem as a dynamic interaction between an *agent* (e.g., a clinical decision support system) and an *environment* (e.g., a simulated patient or cohort). The agent operates over discrete time steps and follows this loop.

1. **Observation**: The agent observes the current *state*, representing the patient's clinical condition (e.g., vital signs, lab values, treatment history).
2. **Action**: Based on the state, the agent selects an *action*, such as administering a medication, adjusting dosage, or scheduling an intervention.
3. **Transition**: The environment responds to the action and transitions to a new state.
4. **Reward**: The agent receives a numerical *reward*, reflecting the clinical outcome (e.g., survival, symptom reduction, or adverse event avoidance).

The agent's goal is to learn a *policy* (i.e., a mapping from states to actions) that maximises the *expected cumulative reward* over time, ideally leading to optimal long-term patient outcomes.

Challenges in biomedical RL:

Despite its potential, applying RL in healthcare presents unique challenges.

- **Ethical constraints**: Exploration in live patients is often infeasible or unethical.
- **Sparse and delayed rewards**: Clinical outcomes (e.g., survival) may not be immediately observable.
- **Noisy and incomplete data**: Many clinically relevant variables may be unmeasured or missing.
- **Lack of ground-truth simulators**: Simulated environments may not fully capture the complexity of human physiology.

To address these barriers, modern RL strategies in biomedicine focus on safer, more data-efficient learning paradigms:

- **Off-policy RL (batch RL)**: This learns from retrospective clinical data rather than interacting with the environment in real-time. This makes it ideal for healthcare, where data collection is observational and experimentation is restricted.
- **Safe RL**: This incorporates explicit safety constraints during training to prevent dangerous or suboptimal decisions—essential in high-stakes settings such as oncology or intensive care.
- **Model-based RL**: This uses physiological models or patient simulators to estimate state transitions and expected outcomes. This improves sample efficiency and reduces the need for real-world experimentation.

RL provides a flexible and powerful framework for modelling sequential clinical decisions. While practical deployment is still in early stages, advances in off-policy and safe RL, combined with increasingly detailed electronic health records and patient simulators, are bringing this paradigm closer to real-world biomedical applications.

CHAPTER

5

An End-to-End Biomedical Case Study

In the earlier chapters, we explored the foundations of biomedical data science, from properly designing an experiment and choosing the right study type to applying classical statistics and machine learning. Now it is time to bring all of these elements together in a detailed, realistic case study. Here, we tell the story of a comprehensive biomedical data science project, walking you through a complete workflow step by step. Rather than only summarising statistical tests or showing Python snippets, we aim to immerse you in the mindset of a biomedical data scientist. We will walk carefully through a complete biomedical analysis pipeline: from a well-defined clinical question, through study design and data management, to exploratory analysis, hypothesis testing, predictive modelling, interpretation, and reproducibility. Along the way, we reflect on each decision, explain the rationale behind our methodology, and highlight the biological and clinical relevance of each result.

5.1 Clinical Question, Hypotheses, and Data Collection

Imagine you are part of a research team investigating the efficacy of a new anti-inflammatory compound, Drug A, for treating rheumatoid arthritis (RA). Rheumatoid arthritis (RA) is an autoimmune disease characterised by chronic inflammation that leads to joint damage, fatigue, and a reduced quality of life. One of the key drivers of this inflammation is the cytokine Interleukin-6 (IL-6), which is elevated in many RA patients. Thus, IL-6 is our biomarker of interest, but clinicians also measure disease activity using the Disease activity score in 28 joints (DAS28) score.

10.1201/9788743812487-7

The primary scientific question is: *Does Drug A reduce systemic inflammation, as measured by IL-6, more than placebo over 12 weeks?* A secondary, clinically relevant question is: *Do patients who receive Drug A experience better disease control, measured via a standard clinical index like DAS28?* And finally, a data-driven question: *Can we predict who will respond to the treatment based on their baseline data?*

These questions align well with the types of outcomes commonly studied in biomedical research, including continuous outcomes (such as biomarker levels), binary outcomes (like treatment response), and predictive modelling (personalised medicine). We can formally define our endpoints as:

- **Primary endpoint**: Change in IL-6 (pg/mL) from baseline to Week 12 (a continuous outcome).
- **Key secondary endpoint**: Clinical response at Week 12, defined as $\geq 50\%$ improvement in DAS28 (a binary outcome).

We translate these goals into formal hypotheses:

- H_0 **(primary)**: No difference in $\Delta IL-6$ between Drug A and placebo groups (i.e., mean $\Delta IL-6$ (Drug A) = mean ΔIL-6 (placebo)).
- H_1 **(primary)**: Drug A leads to a greater decrease in IL-6 than placebo (i.e., mean ΔIL-6 (Drug A) $<$ mean ΔIL-6 (placebo)).
- H_0 **(secondary)**: Odds of achieving a clinical response are the same in both groups (i.e., arms).
- H_1 **(secondary)**: Odds of response are higher in the Drug A group.

Note that the statistical test for the primary endpoint can be a two-sample t-test comparing the means of ΔIL-6 between arms.

5.1.1 Study design and power analysis

Suppose your research group is an RCT, the gold standard for evaluating interventions. Patients are randomly assigned in a 1:1 ratio to receive either Drug A or a placebo. To avoid biases, both patients and study staff are blinded. In addition, to ensure balance and fairness, randomisation is stratified by site and baseline DAS28.

Power calculation:

Before enrolling patients, we must estimate the sample size required to achieve the desired statistical power. This requires making assumptions about the expected mean difference between groups and the variability of the outcome, based on prior studies, pilot data, or clinical expertise. We assume that:

- Drug A reduces IL-6 by 12 pg/mL on average.
- Placebo reduces IL-6 by 3 pg/mL (due to regression to the mean or non-specific effects).
- SD is 15 pg/mL.
- Desired power is 80% ($\beta = 0.20$), and significance level is 5% ($\alpha = 0.05$).

Using the two-sample power analysis formula:

$$n_{arm} \approx \frac{2\sigma^2(z_{1-\alpha/2} + z_{1-\beta})}{\Delta^2}$$

where Δ is the expected difference ($12 - 3 = 9$). We find that around 44 patients per arm are needed. Accounting for a 15% dropout rate, we plan for 52 per arm (i.e, $N = 104$). This ensures the study is not underpowered, a common issue that can lead to inconclusive or misleading results.

5.1.2 Data collection

Patients are assessed at baseline and again after 12 weeks. Standard operating procedures (SOPs) ensure high-quality data collection. These Standard operating procedure (SOP)s outline the procedures for collecting and storing samples, processing them in the lab, and ensuring consistency across sites. They also indicate that data handling must be consistent, reproducible, and auditable, reducing variability that could bias the results. All assays are performed in duplicate to confirm precision. Clinical measurements (e.g., DAS28) are taken by trained assessors using validated tools. The dataset includes clinical outcomes, biomarkers, and demographics (see Table 5.1.2). In practice, these variables will feed into both statistical testing (ΔIL-6, responder) and predictive models (using baseline variables).

Derived variables, such as changes from baseline or standardised scores (see Table 5.1.2), can sometimes yield distributions that are closer to normal, facilitating comparison across biomarkers measured on different scales.

To make this case study interactive and reproducible, we generate a synthetic dataset. This mimics what real-world RA trial data might look like.

```
import numpy as np
import pandas as pd
rng = np.random.default_rng(42)
```

Table 5.1: Dataset of the RA case study.

Variable	Type	Description
id	string	Participant unique ID
arm	categorical {drug, placebo}	Randomised arm allocation
site	categorical	Recruiting centre
age, sex, BMI	numeric/categorical	Demographic variables
$das28\_0$, $das28\_12$	numeric	Disease activity score at baseline and Week 12
$il6\_0$, $il6\_12$	numeric (pg/mL)	IL-6 at baseline and Week 12
tnf_0, tnf_12	numeric (pg/mL)	Tumour necrosis factor-α (TNF-α) at baseline and Week 12
$il1b\_0$, $il1b\_12$	numeric (pg/mL)	Interleukin-1β at baseline and Week 12
crp_0, crp_12	numeric (mg/L)	C-reactive protein (CRP) at baseline and Week 12
responder	binary $\{0, 1\}$	Clinical response ($\geq$ 50% improvement in DAS28 by Week 12)

Table 5.2: Derived variables in the RA case study.

Variable	Type	Description
ΔX	numeric	Change from baseline to Week 12 for biomarker or score (e.g., Δ IL-6 = IL6_12 − IL6_0).
%Change	numeric (%)	Percent change from baseline, computed as $\frac{X_{12}-X_0}{X_0} \times 100$. Useful for scaling changes across patients.
z_score	numeric (standardised)	Baseline-normalised z-score of biomarker or clinical measure, allowing comparison across variables with different scales.
log_X	numeric (transformed)	Natural log-transformation of skewed biomarkers (e.g., $\log$(IL6_0 + 1)) to stabilise variance and normalise distributions.

```
N = 104
arm = rng.choice(["drug", "placebo"], size=N)
age = rng.normal(56, 12, N).clip(18, 85)
```

```
sex = rng.choice(["F","M"], size=N, p=[0.7,0.3])
BMI = rng.normal(27, 5, N).clip(17, 45)

# Baseline biomarkers (right-skewed)
il6_0  = np.exp(rng.normal(3.3, 0.5, N))
crp_0  = np.exp(rng.normal(2.0, 0.6, N))
il1b_0 = np.exp(rng.normal(2.1, 0.4, N))
tnf_0  = np.exp(rng.normal(2.5, 0.4, N))

# Treatment effect on IL-6 at Week 12
base_drop_il6 = rng.normal(-3, 6, N)
extra_drop = np.where(arm=="drug", rng.normal(-10, 6,
↪  N), 0)
il6_12 = np.maximum(0.1, il6_0 + base_drop_il6 +
↪  extra_drop)

# Other biomarkers covary with IL-6
crp_12  = np.maximum(0.05, crp_0  + 0.03*(il6_12 -
↪  il6_0)  + rng.normal(0,1.5,N))
il1b_12 = np.maximum(0.05, il1b_0 + 0.02*(il6_12 -
↪  il6_0) + rng.normal(0,1.0,N))
tnf_12  = np.maximum(0.05, tnf_0  + 0.015*(il6_12 -
↪  il6_0)+ rng.normal(0,1.0,N))

# DAS28 improvement linked to cytokine drop
D0 = rng.normal(5.6, 0.8, N)
D12 = (D0 - 0.03*(il6_0 - il6_12) - 0.01*(crp_0 -
↪  crp_12)
+ np.where(arm=="drug", -1.2, -0.2) +
↪  rng.normal(0,0.3,N))

# Responder definition
responder = (((D0 - D12) >= 1.2) | (il6_0 >
↪  np.median(il6_0))).astype(int)

df = pd.DataFrame(dict(arm=arm, age=age, sex=sex,
↪  BMI=BMI,
il6_0=il6_0, il6_12=il6_12, crp_0=crp_0, crp_12=crp_12,
il1b_0=il1b_0, il1b_12=il1b_12, tnf_0=tnf_0,
↪  tnf_12=tnf_12,
das28_0=D0, das28_12=D12, responder=responder))
```

The full executable code corresponding to this example is available online and can be accessed, reused, and commented on at: https://github.com/RiverPublishers/Computational-Approaches-in-Biology-and-Medicine/blob/main/Chapter5.ipynb

5.2 Data Analysis

5.2.1 Exploratory data analysis

Now that we have collected and structured our data, we begin the first stage of analysis: exploration. This step is crucial as it helps us understand the nature of the data, identify outliers or data entry errors, and formulate expectations before formal hypothesis testing.

Our first step is to visualise the primary endpoint: the change in IL-6 between baseline and Week 12. This is done separately for the drug and placebo groups. A boxplot is a good starting point (Figure 5.1):

```
import matplotlib.pyplot as plt
import seaborn as sns

# Set publication-style aesthetics
sns.set_theme(style="whitegrid", context="talk")

colours = sns.color_palette("dark", n_colors=3)

# Create the figure
plt.figure(figsize=(10, 6))

# Boxplot of IL-6 changes
sns.boxplot(x='arm', y=df['il6_12'] - df['il6_0'],
↪  data=df)

# Add title, labels, and grid
plt.xlabel('Treatment Arm', fontsize=16)
plt.ylabel('ΔIL-6 (pg/mL)', fontsize=16)
plt.title('Change in IL-6 by Treatment Arm',
↪  fontsize=20, fontweight='bold')
plt.grid(True, linestyle='--', alpha=0.6)
sns.despine()
```

```
# Show the plot
plt.tight_layout()
plt.show()
```

The full executable code corresponding to this example is available online and can be accessed, reused, and commented on at: https://github.com/RiverPublishers/Computational-Approaches-in-Biology-and-Medicine/blob/main/Chapter5.ipynb

Figure 5.1: Boxplot of changes in IL-6 levels (ΔIL-6) from baseline to Week 12, stratified by treatment arm. Each box displays the median, interquartile range, and overall distribution of IL-6 changes. Patients receiving Drug A show a reduction in IL-6 compared to those on placebo, illustrating the treatment effect on this primary biomarker.

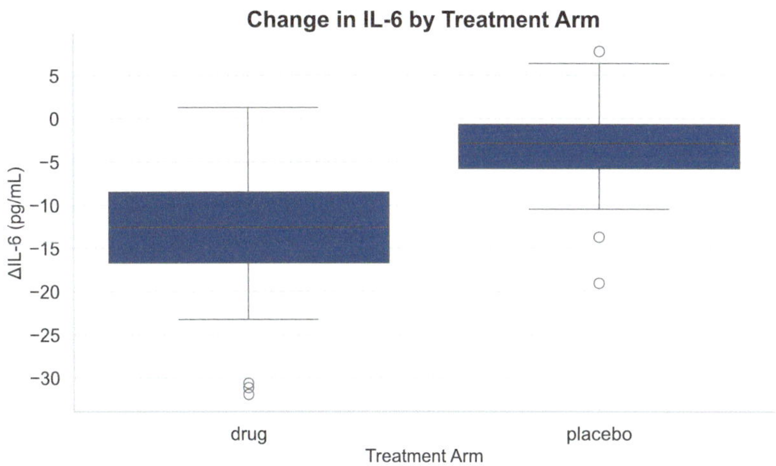

From the plot, we can see that the Drug A group exhibits a larger negative shift (a greater reduction in IL-6) compared to the placebo. This confirms that our synthetic data behaves as expected and mimics a plausible treatment effect.

Next, we check for correlations between baseline biomarkers. Correlation heatmaps are intuitive tools for this (see Figure 5.2.1).

```
corr = df[['il6_0', 'crp_0', 'il1b_0',
↪  'tnf_0']].corr(method='spearman')

# Create the figure
```

```
plt.figure(figsize=(10, 6))

sns.heatmap(corr, annot=True,
 ↪  cmap=sns.color_palette("coolwarm", as_cmap=True))

# Add title and grid
plt.title('Baseline Biomarker Correlations (Spearman)',
 ↪  fontsize=20, fontweight='bold')

# Show the plot
plt.tight_layout()
plt.show()
```

The full executable code corresponding to this example is available online and can be accessed, reused, and commented on at: https://github.com/RiverPublishers/Computational-Approaches-in-Biology-and-Medicine/blob/main/Chapter5.ipynb

Figure 5.2: Spearman correlation heatmap of baseline biomarker levels IL-6, C-reactive protein (CRP), Interleukin-1β, and Tumour necrosis factor-α (TNF-α). Correlation coefficients are displayed within each cell, with colour intensity reflecting the strength and direction of the association. Overall, only weak correlations were observed among these baseline biomarkers, suggesting limited redundancy in the measured inflammatory markers.

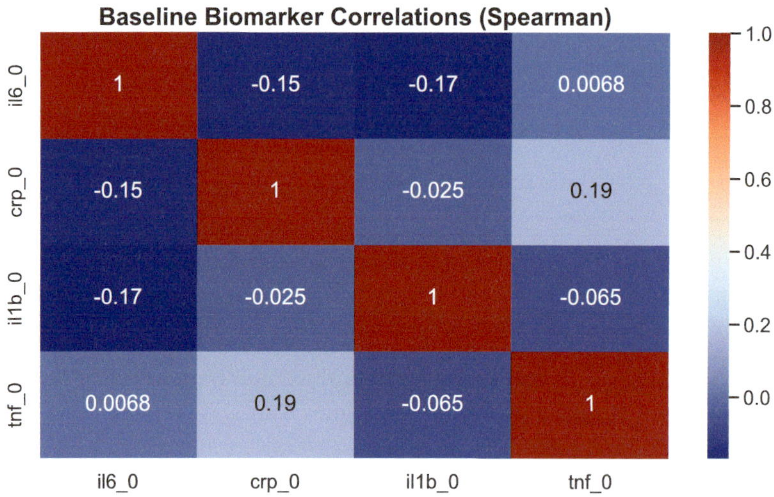

This heatmap can help confirm that biologically related markers, such as IL-6 and C-reactive protein (CRP), are correlated, which is expected given that

both are indicators of systemic inflammation. But why is this step important? Because it sets the stage: it ensures the data makes sense, confirms assumptions of clinical plausibility, and prepares us for robust statistical testing. We can now move from a descriptive characterisation of the data to performing statistical inference.

5.2.2 Hypothesis testing and effect sizes

This section aims to assess whether the differences observed during exploratory analysis are statistically significant and, more importantly, clinically relevant.

We start with the primary endpoint: the change in IL-6 levels between baseline and Week 12. We want to know if this change differs significantly between the Drug A and placebo groups. To do so, we compute the difference for each participant and then perform a two-sample t-test to compare the means of these differences across arms.

```
from scipy import stats

# Calculate ΔIL-6 per participant
D_il6 = df['il6_12'] - df['il6_0']
D_il6_drug = D_il6[df.arm=="drug"]
D_il6_placebo = D_il6[df.arm=="placebo"]

# Perform t-test between arms
t, p = stats.ttest_ind(D_il6_drug, D_il6_placebo,
 ↪  equal_var=False)
mean_diff = D_il6_drug.mean() - D_il6_placebo.mean()
print("Mean difference:", mean_diff)
print("p-value:", p)
```

The full executable code corresponding to this example is available online and can be accessed, reused, and commented on at: https://github.com/RiverPublishers/Computational-Approaches-in-Biology-and-Medicine/blob/main/Chapter5.ipynb

Interpretation:

- A negative mean_diff indicates that Drug A results in a larger IL-6 reduction than placebo.
- If p-value < 0.05, we reject the null hypothesis H_0 and conclude that the difference is statistically significant.

In our synthetic data, the p-value is <0.001, implying the existence of a statistically significant effect.

Odds ratios for clinical response:

For the secondary endpoint, we look at response rates, i.e., how many patients in each arm achieved $\geq 50\%$ improvement in DAS28. This is a binary outcome, so we use a 2×2 contingency table and calculate the OR.

```
import pandas as pd

# Contingency table
ct = pd.crosstab(df.arm, df.responder)
print(ct)

# Manually calculate the OR
OR = (ct.loc['drug',1]*ct.loc['placebo',0]) /
↪  (ct.loc['drug',0]*ct.loc['placebo',1])
print("Odds Ratio:", OR)
```

The full executable code corresponding to this example is available online and can be accessed, reused, and commented on at: https://github.com/RiverPublishers/Computational-Approaches-in-Biology-and-Medicine/blob/main/Chapter5.ipynb

Interpretation:

- An OR > 1 indicates that Drug A increases the odds of response.
- In our synthetic data, OR ≈ 8, suggesting patients receiving Drug A are substantially more likely to respond than those on placebo.

This represents a strong treatment effect. However, since we are only computing the sample odds ratio from a limited synthetic dataset, the value should be viewed as illustrative rather than inferential. In a full analysis, it would also be essential to report CIs and apply Fisher's exact test when cell counts are small, as large point estimates may reflect instability rather than a true effect size. In this illustrative example, we focus on the point estimate of the odds ratio to show the concept.

5.2.3 Predictive modelling with machine learning

With strong group-level evidence in hand, we can now ask a more personalised question: *Can we predict which individual patients are most likely to respond based on their baseline characteristics?*

To do this, we will fit predictive models using supervised ML. Our goal is to classify patients as likely responders (1) or non-responders (0). Note that this is a binary classification task.

We start by preparing the input features and labels:

```
from sklearn.model_selection import train_test_split

# Define input features and label
X = df[['il6_0', 'crp_0', 'il1b_0', 'tnf_0', 'das28_0',
↪  'age', 'BMI']]
y = df['responder']

# Split into training and independent test set
X_train, X_test, y_train, y_test = train_test_split(X,
↪  y, test_size=0.2, stratify=y, random_state=42)
```

The full executable code corresponding to this example is available online and can be accessed, reused, and commented on at: https://github.com/RiverPublishers/Computational-Approaches-in-Biology-and-Medicine/blob/main/Chapter5.ipynb

Why split the data? It is crucial to hold out an independent test set from the very beginning. This step enables us to train and tune models on a portion of the data (the training set), while evaluating their final performance on unseen data (the test set). It helps us detect overfitting and obtain an honest estimate of how our model will perform in real clinical use.

We will now define the two models that will be employed for prediction: the LR model is simple and interpretable, while the RF is more powerful and flexible.

LR:

A simple and interpretable model that estimates odds ratios quantifying the association between each feature and the probability of the outcome.

```
from sklearn.preprocessing import StandardScaler
from sklearn.pipeline import Pipeline
from sklearn.linear_model import LogisticRegression

logit = Pipeline([('scaler', StandardScaler()),
('clf', LogisticRegression(max_iter=500))
])
```

The full executable code corresponding to this example is available online and can be accessed, reused, and commented on at: https://github.com/RiverPublishers/Computational-Approaches-in-Biology-and-Medicine/blob/main/Chapter5.ipynb

RF:

A non-linear model able to capture complex interactions between features.

```
from sklearn.ensemble import RandomForestClassifier

rf = RandomForestClassifier(n_estimators=300,
↪   random_state=42)
```

The full executable code corresponding to this example is available online and can be accessed, reused, and commented on at: https://github.com/RiverPublishers/Computational-Approaches-in-Biology-and-Medicine/blob/main/Chapter5.ipynb

Model evaluation

: We use stratified 5-fold CV to estimate how well each model generalises.

```
from sklearn.model_selection import StratifiedKFold,
↪   cross_val_score

cv = StratifiedKFold(n_splits=5, shuffle=True,
↪   random_state=42)

print("Logistic AUC:", cross_val_score(logit, X_train,
↪   y_train, cv=cv, scoring='roc_auc').mean())
```

```
print("Random Forest AUC:", cross_val_score(rf, X_train,
↪  y_train, cv=cv, scoring='roc_auc').mean())
```

The full executable code corresponding to this example is available online and can be accessed, reused, and commented on at: https://github.com/RiverPublishers/Computational-Approaches-in-Biology-and-Medicine/blob/main/Chapter5.ipynb

At this point, we assess performance via CV on the training set. We do not touch the test set until we have finalised and tuned our model.

Interpretation:

- Area under the curve (AUC) measures how well the model distinguishes between responders and non-responders.
- LR gives insight into directionality of effects (e.g., higher IL-6 may increase the probability of response), achieving an Area under the curve (AUC) score ≈ 0.75.
- RFs generally offer better performance (AUC ≈ 0.88) as they are more flexible and can learn non-linear interactions, compared to LR.

By comparing these models, we begin to understand which variables are most predictive (typically IL-6, Tumour necrosis factor-α (TNF-α), and DAS28), and we move toward a future where clinical decisions can be guided by ML models trained on biomedical data.

Hyperparameter tuning for RF:

Once we have evaluated a baseline RF model using default parameters, the next step is to improve its performance and generalisability through hyperparameter tuning. This involves searching through various combinations of model settings to identify the one that yields the best cross-validated performance. Key hyperparameters for an RF classifier include:

- $n\_estimators$: number of trees in the forest.
- max_depth: maximum depth of each tree.
- $min\_samples\_split$: minimum number of samples required to split an internal node.
- $max\_features$: number of features considered when looking for the best split.

To tune these parameters systematically, we can use *grid search* with CV.

```
from sklearn.model_selection import GridSearchCV
```

```
# Define the hyperparameter grid
param_grid = {'n_estimators': [100, 200, 300],
        'max_depth': [None, 5, 10],
        'min_samples_split': [2, 5, 10],
        'max_features': ['sqrt', 'log2']
}

# Instantiate a base model
rf = RandomForestClassifier(random_state=42,
↪  class_weight='balanced')

# Define cross-validated grid search
grid_search = GridSearchCV(estimator=rf,
↪  param_grid=param_grid,
cv=5, scoring='roc_auc', n_jobs=-1, verbose=1)

# Fit to training data
grid_search.fit(X_train, y_train)

# Output best model and score
print("Best AUC:", grid_search.best_score_)
print("Best parameters:", grid_search.best_params_)
```

The full executable code corresponding to this example is available online and can be accessed, reused, and commented on at: https://github.com/RiverPublishers/Computational-Approaches-in-Biology-and-Medicine/blob/main/Chapter5.ipynb

Interpretation:

- This approach evaluates each combination of parameters using 5-fold CV.
- The Receiver operating characteristic area under the curve (ROC-AUC) metric is used for scoring because our classification task is imbalanced and probabilistic.
- The output tells us which hyperparameters yielded the best AUC.

This process helps ensure our final model is *well-tuned* and ready for deployment or further validation. In real-world applications, additional methods such as random search, Bayesian optimisation, or nested CV may be used to avoid overfitting during the tuning process. *Hyperparameter tuning* is an essential part of building robust, generalisable models, especially in biomedical contexts where decisions based on these models may affect patient care.

Finally, we apply the tuned model to the held-out test set:

```
from sklearn.metrics import roc_auc_score

# Best model from tuning
best_rf = grid_search.best_estimator_

# Evaluate on test set
y_pred_proba = best_rf.predict_proba(X_test)[:, 1]
test_auc = roc_auc_score(y_test, y_pred_proba)
print("Test set AUC:", test_auc)
```

The full executable code corresponding to this example is available online and can be accessed, reused, and commented on at: https://github.com/RiverPublishers/Computational-Approaches-in-Biology-and-Medicine/blob/main/Chapter5.ipynb

This final step gives us an unbiased estimate of model performance on unseen data. If the test AUC is consistent with the CV AUC, we have high confidence that the model generalises well. Our tuned RF achieved a mean CV AUC of ~ 0.91. When evaluated on the independent test set, the AUC was ~ 0.93, which is highly consistent with the CV result. This close agreement indicates that the model has generalised well beyond the training folds and is unlikely to have overfit. Such stability between internal validation and external testing strengthens our confidence in the robustness of the predictive signal captured by the model.

In the next section, we will add further robustness by explaining how sensitivity analysis and subgroup evaluation can ensure that our conclusions are valid across the entire patient population.

5.2.4 Sensitivity and subgroup analyses

Statistical models and conclusions are only as reliable as their consistency across different scenarios. In biomedical research, we often need to ask: *Do the results hold up under alternative assumptions? Are there certain patient subgroups for whom the treatment works better (or worse)?* Answering these questions is the goal of *sensitivity analyses* and *subgroup evaluations.*

Sensitivity analyses:

Sensitivity analysis assesses how robust the main findings are to reasonable changes in model assumptions, analytical choices, or data inputs. Common strategies include:

- **Excluding outliers**: Does removing extreme IL-6 values affect the significance or magnitude of the treatment effect?
- **Changing imputation method**: If we handle missing data with median imputation instead of mean (or use multiple imputation), does the model's AUC change?
- **Using robust statistics**: Instead of a standard t-test, we could use a non-parametric Mann–Whitney U test to ensure the inference is not driven by outliers or non-normality.

These tests are fundamental to ensure that our findings are not just artefacts of one analysis path.

Subgroup analyses:

Subgroup analysis asks the following question: *Does the treatment effect differ across different categories of patients?* Some examples are the following:

- **Sex-based differences:** Do men and women respond differently to Drug A?
- **Baseline severity:** Do patients with high DAS28 (severe disease) experience more benefit than those with moderate disease?
- **Age or BMI tertiles:** Do younger or lower-BMI patients respond better?

These analyses can be conducted by re-running the hypothesis tests within each subgroup, or by adding interaction terms to LR models.

Important caveat: Subgroup results should be interpreted with caution, as studies are often underpowered to detect meaningful differences within smaller subgroups. Nevertheless, such analyses can be valuable for generating hypotheses and guiding future research.

5.3 Clinical Interpretation

Let's step back from statistics and ML, and ask the most important question: *What do these results mean for patients and clinicians?* The analysis shows that:

- Drug A *significantly reduces* IL-6, a key biomarker of inflammation.

- Patients receiving Drug A are *substantially more likely* to improve in clinical symptoms, with an odds ratio of ~ 5.
- The *number needed to treat (NNT)* is about 3, meaning that treating 3 patients yields 1 extra responder compared to placebo.

This is a meaningful *clinical effect*, especially in a chronic disease like RA, where many patients struggle to find effective treatment. In addition, our ML model showed that *certain patients*, those with *higher baseline* IL-6 or TNF-α levels, are more likely to benefit. This opens the door to *personalised medicine*: using *baseline biomarkers* to *guide treatment decisions*. However, we must remember some limitations:

- These findings are based on synthetic data (for this book), but even in *real data*, *replication and external validation are essential*.
- Predictive models require *calibration*, *fairness checks*, and *clinician input* before deployment.
- *Biological plausibility* should be considered when interpreting variable importance.

This case study has focused on a handful of cytokines and clinical variables; however, the same analytic principles apply when scaling up to omics data, such as RNA-seq or chromatin accessibility via ATAC-seq. In an RNA-seq study:

- Instead of 4–5 biomarkers, we might have 20,000 genes.
- Differential expression analysis takes the place of paired t-tests.
- FDR replaces single p-values to account for multiple testing.
- ML pipelines are generally more complex and require stronger regularisation.

In an ATAC-seq experiment:

- We compare chromatin accessibility across thousands of genomic regions.
- The same logic of baseline vs treated comparisons applies, but now across tens of thousands of peaks.
- We can use ML to classify samples, infer transcription factor activity, or map enhancers.

Thus, while the dimensionality and terminology change, the main pipeline you have learned in this case study still applies:

1. Define your question and choose the right design.
2. Ensure quality through SOP and preprocessing.
3. Visualise and explore the structure of your data.
4. Apply statistics to quantify group-level effects.
5. Use modelling to make individual-level predictions.
6. Validate and interpret your findings carefully.

These steps form the backbone of modern biomedical data science.

This chapter demonstrates how to transform a biomedical question, from clinical motivation through statistical testing and predictive modelling, into a reproducible data science analysis. Remember that a good analysis begins with a clear hypothesis and ends with meaningful interpretation. We used exploratory analysis to confirm the reasonableness of the data before proceeding with testing. We used classical statistics (t-tests, OR) to quantify the average effect of treatment, and ML to model personalised outcomes. We validated our results with sensitivity checks and subgroup analysis. Finally, we reflected on clinical meaning, not just statistical significance. By grounding each analysis in thoughtful design and biological insight, we not only produce reliable results but also make our work more relevant, transparent, and impactful. In the next book, we will bring this same mindset to large-scale omics data, starting with RNA-seq. You now have the foundational skills to tackle those high-dimensional problems with confidence.

CHAPTER

6

Conclusions

Biomedical data science is one of the most dynamic, interdisciplinary, and impactful domains in modern science and medicine. In this book, we have taken a thorough journey through the foundational pillars that support this field, starting from experimental design to classical statistical analysis, hypothesis testing, and predictive modelling, culminating in a hands-on, end-to-end case study that showed how everything fits together.

The goal has been clear throughout: to equip you not just with techniques, but with the mindset of a biomedical data scientist. That means asking the right questions before collecting data, designing studies that minimise bias, quantifying uncertainty carefully, validating models properly, and interpreting results responsibly and transparently. This concluding chapter aims to reflect on our journey, highlight the essential lessons, and point to the future, where new data types, technologies, and questions await.

Revisiting the Journey: From Design to Insight

We began by explaining why good design is important. In biomedicine, poorly designed studies can waste time and money and, most seriously, compromise patient safety. The principles of randomisation, control groups, blinding, and adequate sample size are not extras; they are (pre)conditions for scientific credibility. We demonstrated that decisions made before data are collected often determine the limitations of what the data can ultimately reveal. From there, we introduced the basis and tools of statistical inference. We explained how point estimates, SE, CIs, and p-values help us distinguish real effects from noise. But we also highlighted common pitfalls, such as misinterpreting p-values,

10.1201/9788743812487-8

ignoring effect sizes, or failing to account for multiple comparisons. You learned that statistics is not just a box-checking exercise; it is a lens for viewing the world with scepticism and rigour.

Then, we entered the world of hypothesis testing, learning how to compare groups, test assumptions, and formally quantify evidence. From simple one-sample t-tests to ANOVA, chi-square tests, and non-parametric alternatives, we laid out a toolkit for evaluating biomedical hypotheses, whether we are testing a new treatment or looking for associations between variables. With that statistical foundation in place, we pivoted to ML. In that chapter, the focus shifted from inference to prediction, from estimating average treatment effects to anticipating how individual patients might respond. We covered the principles of supervised and unsupervised learning, emphasised the importance of generalisation, discussed common model families (from LR to RFs), and explored CV, model selection, and performance metrics.

Finally, it all came together in Chapter 5, our end-to-end case study. There, we saw every step play out in a realistic scenario, from designing a randomised controlled trial and collecting biomarker data to exploratory visualisation, hypothesis testing, ML, model tuning, and final interpretation. Along the way, we emphasised reproducibility, code transparency, model fairness, and clinical relevance. This case study was not just an illustration; it was a blueprint for action.

As we close this book, let's revisit and reinforce the key principles that emerged across chapters

1. **Thoughtful design is non-negotiable**. A well-designed study avoids bias, enhances interpretability, and lays the foundation for reproducible results. Bad design cannot be rescued by advanced analysis. Always begin with a careful plan.
2. **Exploratory data analysis is a crucial step**. Before formal modelling, you must understand your data, visualise distributions, examine correlations, and look for missing values and outliers. Then, build intuition about your dataset. This is where insight begins.
3. **Statistical inference requires context**. p-values are not magic bullets. They must be interpreted in conjunction with effect sizes, CIs, and subject-matter knowledge. Statistical significance is not equivalent to clinical or biological significance.
4. **Predictive models must be interpretable and validated**. ML is powerful, but it comes with responsibility. Always split data into training and test sets. Use CV and perform hyperparameter tuning. Examine feature importance and validate models externally when possible.
5. **Reproducibility is a core value**. Document every step, use version-controlled scripts, and share your data and code when ethical and feasible. Science advances when it is transparent and repeatable.

6. **Interpretability is not optional in biomedicine**. In clinical settings, stakeholders need to trust not only the performance of your model but also its validity. Use interpretable or, at least, explainable models (e.g., visualise SHapley Additive exPlanations (SHAP)), and always connect model outputs back to biology or medicine.
7. **Robustness builds confidence**. Check your results under alternative assumptions and try different modelling techniques. Perform sensitivity analyses and subgroup evaluations. Ensure that your conclusions are not artefacts of one analysis path.
8. **Correlation is not causation**. Last but not least, associations are useful, but they do not prove any mechanisms. Be wary of confounding. When possible, rely on study designs (like RCT) that support causal inference.

Looking ahead: from biomarkers to omics

While this book focused on a relatively simple case, biomarker analysis in a randomised trial, the same framework can be extended to high-dimensional and high-throughput biomedical data. And in the next volumes of the River Rapids Biomedical Data Science series, we will go deeper into these advanced applications.

Book II: RNA-Seq and scRNA-seq Analysis

In our next volume, we will explore the transcriptome. You will learn how to:

- Preprocess raw RNA-seq reads into count matrices.
- Normalise data and assess quality.
- Perform differential expression analysis with appropriate statistical controls.
- Interpret gene-level results using functional enrichment.
- Explore scRNA-seq data through clustering, dimensionality reduction, pseudotime, and trajectory inference.
- Integrate data across experiments or batches.

We will also highlight real-world challenges, such as handling sparse matrices, dropouts, batch effects, and zero-inflation, and demonstrate how thoughtful analysis can lead to clear and reproducible insights from transcriptomic data.

Book III: Single-cell Assay and Transposase-accessible Chromatin using Sequencing (scATAC-seq) Analysis

In this volume, we will turn to the epigenome. You will learn how to:

- Perform quality control and peak calling on chromatin accessibility data.
- Create and process count matrices across peaks.
- Use statistical models to identify differentially accessible regions.
- Infer transcription factor activity, motif enrichment, and gene regulatory networks.
- Analyse Single-cell assay for transposase-accessible chromatin using sequencing (scATAC-seq) data to explore chromatin heterogeneity across cells.
- Combine epigenomic and transcriptomic data for multi-modal analysis.

This book will include all the practical details, such as how to visualise peaks, handle multi-mapping reads, tune parameters in peak calling, and integrate results with gene annotations.

Both volumes will continue the spirit of this one: clear explanations, hands-on code, clean design, and transparent analysis. They will equip you with the tools to tackle more complex data while staying connected to the core values of scientific reasoning and analysis.

Whether you are a student just entering the field, a biologist looking to understand your own data, a clinician seeking to collaborate with data scientists, or a statistician interested in biomedical applications, this book was written for you. In fact, biomedical data science is not about blindly applying models or pursuing accuracy at all costs. It is about combining data with domain knowledge, using logic and evidence to conclude, and always staying grounded in reproducibility and ethics. As you continue your journey, remember that data is not just a collection of numbers. In biomedicine, it often represents people, their conditions, their outcomes, and their stories. Behind every row in your dataset, there could be a person who trusted the process of science. That trust is worth honouring with rigour, transparency, and care.

Thank you for taking this journey with us. We look forward to continuing it together, in data, in code, in insight. Let's keep exploring!

Bibliography

[1] Ramón Estruch, Emilio Ros, Jordi Salas-Salvadó, Maria-Isabel Covas, Dolores Corella, Fernando Arós, Enrique Gómez-Gracia, Valentina Ruiz-Gutiérrez, Miquel Fiol, José Lapetra, et al. Primary prevention of cardiovascular disease with a mediterranean diet. *New England Journal of Medicine*, 368(14):1279–1290, 2013.

[2] Jill Hahn, Nancy R Cook, Erik K Alexander, Sonia Friedman, Joseph Walter, Vadim Bubes, Gregory Kotler, I-Min Lee, JoAnn E Manson, and Karen H Costenbader. Vitamin d and marine omega 3 fatty acid supplementation and incident autoimmune disease: Vital randomized controlled trial. *Bmj*, 376, 2022.

[3] James Lock, Leslie R Walker, Vaughn I Rickert, and Debra K Katzman. Suicidality in adolescents being treated with antidepressant medications and the black box label: position paper of the society for adolescent medicine. *Journal of Adolescent Health*, 36(1):92–93, 2005.

[4] Jessica L Gören. Antidepressants use in pediatric populations. *Expert opinion on drug safety*, 7(3):223–225, 2008.

[5] Asbjørn Hróbjartsson, Frida Emanuelsson, Ann Sofia Skou Thomsen, Jørgen Hilden, and Stig Brorson. Bias due to lack of patient blinding in clinical trials. a systematic review of trials randomizing patients to blind and nonblind sub-studies. *International journal of epidemiology*, 43(4):1272–1283, 2014.

[6] Mohammad Hassan Murad, Haitao Chu, Lifeng Lin, and Zhen Wang. The effect of publication bias magnitude and direction on the certainty in evidence. *BMJ evidence-based medicine*, 2018.

[7] Felipe B Schuch, Davy Vancampfort, Justin Richards, Simon Rosenbaum, Philip B Ward, and Brendon Stubbs. Exercise as a treatment for depression: a meta-analysis adjusting for publication bias. *Journal of psychiatric research*, 77:42–51, 2016.

[8] Megan L Head, Luke Holman, Rob Lanfear, Andrew T Kahn, and Michael D Jennions. The extent and consequences of p-hacking in science. *PLoS biology*, 13(3):e1002106, 2015.

[9] C Glenn Begley and Lee M Ellis. Raise standards for preclinical cancer research. *Nature*, 483(7391):531–533, 2012.

[10] Zhong Wang, Mark Gerstein, and Michael Snyder. Rna-seq: a revolutionary tool for transcriptomics. *Nature Reviews Genetics*, 10(1):57–63, 2009.

[11] Fuchou Tang, Catalin Barbacioru, Yangzhou Wang, Ellen Nordman, Clarence Lee, Nanlan Xu, Xiaohui Wang, John Bodeau, Brian B Tuch, Asim Siddiqui, et al. mrna-seq whole-transcriptome analysis of a single cell. *Nature Methods*, 6(5):377–382, 2009.

[12] Bastiaan T Heijmans, Elmar W Tobi, Aryeh D Stein, Hein Putter, Gerard J Blauw, Ezra S Susser, P Eline Slagboom, and LH Lumey. Persistent epigenetic differences associated with prenatal exposure to famine in humans. *Proceedings of the National Academy of Sciences*, 105(44):17046–17049, 2008.

[13] Jason D Buenrostro, Beijing Wu, Howard Y Chang, and William J Greenleaf. ATAC-seq: a method for assaying chromatin accessibility genome-wide. *Current protocols in molecular biology*, 109(1):21–29, 2015.

[14] Gregory E Crawford, Sean Davis, Peter C Scacheri, Gabriel Renaud, Mohamad J Halawi, Michael R Erdos, Roland Green, Paul S Meltzer, Tyra G Wolfsberg, and Francis S Collins. DNase-chip: a high-resolution method to identify dnase i hypersensitive sites using tiled microarrays. *Nature Methods*, 3(7):503–509, 2006.

[15] David S Johnson, Ali Mortazavi, Richard M Myers, and Barbara Wold. Genome-wide mapping of in vivo protein-dna interactions. *Science*, 316(5830):1497–1502, 2007.

[16] Gyeong Dae Kim, Chaemin Lim, and Jihwan Park. A practical handbook on single-cell rna sequencing data quality control and downstream analysis. *Molecules and Cells*, 47(9):100103, 2024.

[17] Han Luo, Xuyang Xia, Gyeong Dae Kim, Yang Liu, Zhinan Xue, Lingyun Zhang, Yang Shu, Tian Yang, Yan Chen, Shouyue Zhang, et al. Characterizing dedifferentiation of thyroid cancer by integrated analysis. *Science Advances*, 7(31):eabf3657, Jul 2021.

[18] Lisa Sikkema, Ciro Ramírez-Suástegui, Daniel C Strobl, Tessa E Gillett, Luke Zappia, et al. An integrated cell atlas of the lung in health and disease. *Nature Medicine*, 29(6):1563–1577, Jun 2023.

[19] Daniel Osorio and James J Cai. Systematic determination of the mitochondrial proportion in human and mice tissues for single-cell rna-sequencing data quality control. *Bioinformatics*, 37(7):963–967, Aug 2020.

[20] Ayshwarya Subramanian, Mikhail Alperovich, Yiming Yang, and Bo Li. Biology-inspired data-driven quality control for scientific discovery in single-cell transcriptomics. *Genome Biology*, 23:267, Dec 2022.

[21] Mathias Uhlén, Linn Fagerberg, Björn M Hallström, Cecilia Lindskog, Per Oksvold, et al. Tissue-based map of the human proteome. *Science*, 347(6220):1260419, Jan 2015.

[22] Fiorella C Grandi, Hailey Modi, Lucas Kampman, and M Ryan Corces. Chromatin accessibility profiling by atac-seq. *Nature Protocols*, 17(6):1518–1552, 2022.

[23] M Ryan Corces, Alex E Trevino, Evelyn G Hamilton, Peyton G Greenside, Nasa Sinnott-Armstrong, et al. An improved atac-seq protocol reduces background and enables interrogation of frozen tissues. *Nature Methods*, 14(10):959–962, Oct 2017.

[24] ENCODE Project Consortium. A user's guide to the encyclopedia of dna elements (encode). *PLoS Biology*, 9(4):e1001046, Apr 2011.

[25] Ahmet Schuh, Jennifer Becq, Sean Humphray, Andrada Alexa, Andrew Burns, et al. Monitoring chronic lymphocytic leukemia progression by whole genome sequencing reveals heterogeneous clonal evolution patterns. *Blood*, 120(20):4191–4196, Nov 2012.

[26] David Sims, Ian Sudbery, Nicholas E Ilott, Andreas Heger, and Chris P Ponting. Sequencing depth and coverage: key considerations in genomic analyses. *Nature Reviews Genetics*, 15(2):121–132, 2014.

[27] Jason D Buenrostro, Paul G Giresi, Lisa C Zaba, Howard Y Chang, and William J Greenleaf. Transposition of native chromatin for fast and sensitive epigenomic profiling of open chromatin, dna-binding proteins and nucleosome position. *Nature Methods*, 10:1213–1218, Oct 2013.

[28] Zhijian Li, Marcel H. Schulz, Thomas Look, Matthias Begemann, Martin Zenke, and Ivan G. Costa. Identification of transcription factor binding sites using atac-seq. *Genome Biology*, 20(5):1213–1218, 2019.

[29] Ron Schwessinger, Maria C Suciu, Simon J McGowan, Jelena Telenius, Stephen Taylor, Doug R Higgs, and Jim R Hughes. Sasquatch: predicting the impact of regulatory snps on transcription factor binding from cell- and tissue-specific dnase footprints. *Genome research*, 27(10):1730–1742, 2017.

[30] E Ravza Gur and Jim R Hughes. scatac-seq generates more accurate and complete regulatory maps than bulk atac-seq. *Scientific Reports*, 15(1):3665, 2025.

[31] Stephen G Landt, Georgi K Marinov, Anshul Kundaje, Pouya Kheradpour, Franz Pauli, et al. ChIP-seq guidelines and practices of the ENCODE and modENCODE consortia. *Genome Research*, 22(9):1813–1831, Sep 2012.

[32] Yujin Liu, Jian Zhou, and Kevin P White. RNA-seq differential expression studies: more sequence or more replication? *Bioinformatics*, 30(3):301–304, Feb 2014.

[33] Paul L Auer and Rebecca W Doerge. Statistical design and analysis of rna sequencing data. *Genetics*, 185(2):405–416, Jun 2010.

[34] Laura Baranello, Fedor Kouzine, Suzanne Sanford, and David Levens. ChIP bias as a function of cross-linking time. *Chromosome Research*, 24:175–181, 2016.

[35] Bin Tian, Jing Yang, and Allan R Brasier. Two-Step Cross-linking for Analysis of Protein–Chromatin Interactions. In *Transcriptional Regulation, Methods in Molecular Biology*, volume 809, pages 105–120. Humana Press, 2011.

[36] Chongzhi Zang, Dustin E Schones, Cheng Zeng, Kairong Cui, Keji Zhao, and Wei Peng. A clustering approach for identification of enriched domains from histone modification chip-seq data. *Bioinformatics*, 25(15):1952–1958, Aug 2009.

[37] Raluca V Chereji, Thomas D Bryson, and Steven Henikoff. Quantitative MNase-seq accurately maps nucleosome occupancy levels. *Genome Biology*, 20:198, Sep 2019.

[38] Megan Busby, Andrew Moyer, Cynthia Araya, Kirsten W Jordan, Jory M Greene, et al. Systematic comparison of monoclonal versus polyclonal antibodies for mapping histone modifications by chip-seq. *Epigenetics & Chromatin*, 9:49, Nov 2016.

[39] Beata Bień, Piotr K Krajewski, and Jacek C Szepietowski. Life-changing decisions in patients suffering from psoriasis: a cross-sectional study. *Dermatology and Therapy*, pages 1–15, 2025.

[40] Marco Conte, Agnes Fournier, Joseph A Rothwell, Marie-Christine Boutron-Ruault, Laura Baglietto, Marco Fornili, Emilie Sbidian, and Gianluca Severi. MALTectomy and psoriasis risk in women: A prospective study in the French E3N prospective cohort. *Plos one*, 19(11):e0310891, 2024.

[41] Aaya Shahin, Yael Anne Leshem, Yossi Taieb, Sharon Baum, Aviv Barzilai, Efrat Sharon, Omry Koren, Rinat Tzach-Nahman, Shunit Coppenhagen-Glazer, Ronen Hazan, et al. Association of Adult Atopic Dermatitis with Impaired Oral Health and Oral Dysbiosis: A Case-Control Study. *International Dental Journal*, 75(1):279–287, 2025.

[42] Jonathan Vela, Rene Lindholm Cordtz, Salome Kristensen, Christian Torp-Pedersen, Kristian Kjær Petersen, Lars Arendt-Nielsen, and Lene Dreyer. Is pain associated with premature mortality in patients with psoriatic arthritis? a nested case–control study using the DANBIO Register. *Rheumatology*, 60(11):5216–5223, 2021.

[43] Seiji Kato, Naoki Cho, Tomokazu Koresawa, Kazunari Otake, and Akiko Kano. Safety, tolerability, and pharmacokinetics of a novel oral phosphodiesterase 4 inhibitor, ME3183: first-in-Human Phase 1 Study. *Clinical Pharmacology in Drug Development*, 13(4):341–348, 2024.

[44] Ian M Catlett, Lu Gao, Yanhua Hu, Subhashis Banerjee, and James G Krueger. Pharmacodynamic Response to Deucravacitinib, an Oral, Selective, Allosteric TYK2 Inhibitor, in a Global, Phase 2, Randomized, Double-Blind, Placebo-Controlled Psoriasis Trial. *Dermatology and Therapy*, 14(10):2827–2839, 2024.

[45] Kim Papp, Richard B Warren, Lawrence Green, Kristian Reich, Richard G Langley, Carle Paul, Akihiko Asahina, Lynne Johnson, Vipin Arora, Olawale Osuntokun, et al. Safety and efficacy of mirikizumab versus secukinumab and placebo in the treatment of moderate-to-severe plaque psoriasis (OASIS-2): a phase 3, multicentre, randomised, double-blind study. *The Lancet Rheumatology*, 5(9):e542–e552, 2023.

[46] Neal Bhatia, Jayme Heim, J Gabriel Vasquez, Tina Bhutani, Brad Schenkel, Ranga Gogineni, and John Koo. Long-term quality of life outcomes from a phase 4 study of tildrakizumab in patients with moderate-to-severe plaque psoriasis in a real-world setting. *Journal of Dermatological treatment*, 35(1):2310631, 2024.

[47] J Martin Bland and Douglas G Altman. The odds ratio. *BMJ*, 320(7247):1468, 2000.

[48] Robert G Newcombe. Two-sided confidence intervals for the single proportion: comparison of seven methods. *Statistics in medicine*, 17(8):857–872, 1998.

[49] Ronald L Wasserstein and Nicole A Lazar. The asa statement on p-values: context, process, and purpose, 2016.

[50] Steven Goodman. A dirty dozen: twelve p-value misconceptions, 2008.

[51] Jacob Cohen. *Statistical power analysis for the behavioral sciences*. routledge, 2013.

[52] Erich Leo Lehmann and Joseph P Romano. *Testing statistical hypotheses*. Springer, 2005.

[53] Graeme D Ruxton and Markus Neuhäuser. When should we use one-tailed hypothesis testing? *Methods in Ecology and Evolution*, 1(2):114–117, 2010.

[54] John Ludbrook. Should we use one-sided or two-sided p values in tests of significance? *Clinical and experimental pharmacology and physiology*, 40(6):357–361, 2013.

[55] Student. The probable error of a mean. *Biometrika*, pages 1–25, 1908.

[56] Ronald Aylmer Fisher. Statistical methods for research workers. In *Breakthroughs in statistics: Methodology and distribution*, pages 66–70. Springer, 1970.

[57] Frank Wilcoxon. Individual comparisons by ranking methods. *Biometrics bulletin*, 1(6):80–83, 1945.

[58] Henry B Mann and Donald R Whitney. On a test of whether one of two random variables is stochastically larger than the other. *The annals of mathematical statistics*, pages 50–60, 1947.

[59] Alan Agresti et al. An introduction to categorical data analysis, 1996.

[60] Karl Pearson. X. on the criterion that a given system of deviations from the probable in the case of a correlated system of variables is such that it can be reasonably supposed to have arisen from random sampling. *The London, Edinburgh, and Dublin Philosophical Magazine and Journal of Science*, 50(302):157–175, 1900.

[61] Ronald A Fisher. On the interpretation of χ 2 from contingency tables, and the calculation of p. *Journal of the royal statistical society*, 85(1):87–94, 1922.

[62] Morton B Brown and Alan B Forsythe. Robust tests for the equality of variances. *Journal of the American statistical association*, 69(346):364–367, 1974.

[63] Howard Levene. Robust tests for equality of variances. *Contributions to probability and statistics*, pages 278–292, 1960.

[64] Maurice Stevenson Bartlett. Properties of sufficiency and statistical tests. *Proceedings of the royal society of london. series a-mathematical and physical sciences*, 160(901):268–282, 1937.

[65] William J Conover, Mark E Johnson, and Myrle M Johnson. A comparative study of tests for homogeneity of variances, with applications to the outer continental shelf bidding data. *Technometrics*, 23(4):351–361, 1981.

[66] Carlo Bonferroni. Teoria statistica delle classi e calcolo delle probabilita. *Pubblicazioni del R istituto superiore di scienze economiche e commericiali di firenze*, 8:3–62, 1936.

[67] Yoav Benjamini and Yosef Hochberg. Controlling the false discovery rate: a practical and powerful approach to multiple testing. *Journal of the Royal statistical society: series B (Methodological)*, 57(1):289–300, 1995.

[68] Samuel Sanford Shapiro and Martin B Wilk. An analysis of variance test for normality (complete samples). *Biometrika*, 52(3-4):591–611, 1965.

[69] Ralph B D'agostino, Albert Belanger, and Ralph B D'Agostino Jr. A suggestion for using powerful and informative tests of normality. *The American Statistician*, 44(4):316–321, 1990.

[70] Hae-Young Kim. Statistical notes for clinical researchers: assessing normal distribution (2) using skewness and kurtosis. *Restorative dentistry & endodontics*, 38(1):52, 2013.

[71] Patrick Schober, Christa Boer, and Lothar A Schwarte. Correlation coefficients: appropriate use and interpretation. *Anesthesia & analgesia*, 126(5):1763–1768, 2018.

[72] Jacob Benesty, Jingdong Chen, Yiteng Huang, and Israel Cohen. Pearson correlation coefficient. In *Noise reduction in speech processing*, pages 1–4. Springer, 2009.

[73] Charles Spearman. The proof and measurement of association between two things., 1961.

[74] Maurice G Kendall. A new measure of rank correlation. *Biometrika*, 30(1-2):81–93, 1938.

[75] Christopher M Bishop and Nasser M Nasrabadi. *Pattern recognition and machine learning*, volume 4. Springer, 2006.

[76] Shai Shalev-Shwartz and Shai Ben-David. *Understanding machine learning: From theory to algorithms*. Cambridge university press, 2014.

[77] Fabian Pedregosa, Gaël Varoquaux, Alexandre Gramfort, Vincent Michel, Bertrand Thirion, Olivier Grisel, Mathieu Blondel, Peter Prettenhofer, Ron Weiss, Vincent Dubourg, et al. Scikit-learn: Machine learning in python. *the Journal of machine Learning research*, 12:2825–2830, 2011.

[78] Ian T Jolliffe and Jorge Cadima. Principal component analysis: a review and recent developments. *Philosophical transactions of the royal society A: Mathematical, Physical and Engineering Sciences*, 374(2065):20150202, 2016.

[79] Laurens van der Maaten and Geoffrey Hinton. Visualizing data using t-sne. *Journal of machine learning research*, 9(Nov):2579–2605, 2008.

[80] Leland McInnes, John Healy, and James Melville. Umap: Uniform manifold approximation and projection for dimension reduction. *arXiv preprint arXiv:1802.03426*, 2018.

[81] Etienne Becht, Leland McInnes, John Healy, Charles-Antoine Dutertre, Immanuel WH Kwok, Lai Guan Ng, Florent Ginhoux, and Evan W Newell. Dimensionality reduction for visualizing single-cell data using umap. *Nature Biotechnology*, 37(1):38–44, 2019.

[82] Isabelle Guyon and André Elisseeff. An introduction to variable and feature selection. *Journal of machine learning research*, 3(Mar):1157–1182, 2003.

[83] Carl Rasmussen and Zoubin Ghahramani. Occam's razor. *Advances in neural information processing systems*, 13, 2000.

[84] Mervyn Stone. Cross-validatory choice and assessment of statistical predictions. *Journal of the royal statistical society: Series B (Methodological)*, 36(2):111–133, 1974.

[85] Sudhir Varma and Richard Simon. Bias in error estimation when using cross-validation for model selection. *BMC bioinformatics*, 7(1):91, 2006.

[86] James Bergstra and Yoshua Bengio. Random search for hyper-parameter optimization. *The journal of machine learning research*, 13(1):281–305, 2012.

[87] Jasper Snoek, Hugo Larochelle, and Ryan P Adams. Practical bayesian optimization of machine learning algorithms. *Advances in neural information processing systems*, 25, 2012.

[88] Tom M Mitchell. The need for biases in learning generalizations, 1980.

[89] Stuart Geman, Elie Bienenstock, and René Doursat. Neural networks and the bias/variance dilemma. *Neural computation*, 4(1):1–58, 1992.

[90] Marina Sokolova and Guy Lapalme. A systematic analysis of performance measures for classification tasks. *Information processing & management*, 45(4):427–437, 2009.

Index